The art of
preserving

The art of
preserving

Ancient techniques and modern inventions
to capture every season in a jar

Emma Macdonald

with Susanna Tee

NOURISH

EAT WELL, LIVE WELL

To all those out there who love to make a good pickle.

The Art of Preserving
Emma Macdonald

First published in the UK as *Bay Tree Preserving*
and in the USA as *Artisan Preserving* in 2014
by Nourish, an imprint of Watkins Media Limited
Unit 11, Shepperton House, 83–93 Shepperton Road,
London N1 3DF

This edition published in 2021 by Nourish

enquiries@nourishbooks.com

PUBLISHER: Grace Cheetham
PROJECT EDITORS: Rebecca Woods and Ella Chappell
EDITORS: Becky Alexander and Sarah Epton
HEAD OF DESIGN: Glen Wilkins
PHOTOGRAPHIC ART DIRECTION: Gail Jones
COMMISSIONED PHOTOGRAPHY: Toby Scott
FOOD STYLIST: Susanna Tee
PROP STYLIST: Lucy Harvey
PRODUCTION: Uzma Taj

A CIP record for this book is available from
the British Library

ISBN: 978-1-84899-398-3 (Hardback)
ISBN: 978-1-84899-399-0 (eBook)

10 9 8 7 6 5 4 3 2 1

Typeset in Freight Sans and Lust Display

Printed in China

Publisher's note

While every care has been taken in compiling the recipes
for this book, Watkins Media Limited, or any other persons
who have been involved in working on this publication,
cannot accept responsibility for any errors or omissions,
inadvertent or not, that may be found in the recipes or text,
nor for any problems that may arise as a result of preparing
one of these recipes. If you are pregnant or breastfeeding
or have any special dietary requirements or medical
conditions, it is advisable to consult a medical professional
before following any of the recipes contained in this book.
Ill or elderly people, babies, young children, and women
who are pregnant or breastfeeding should avoid recipes
containing raw meat or fish or uncooked eggs.

NOTES ON THE RECIPES

Unless otherwise stated:

- Use medium fruit and vegetables

- Use medium (US large) organic or free-range eggs

- Use fresh herbs, spices and chillies

- Use granulated sugar (Americans can use ordinary granulated sugar when caster sugar is specified)

- Do not mix metric, imperial and US cup measurements: 1 tsp = 5ml 1 tbsp = 15ml 1 cup = 250ml

nourishbooks.com

Contents

Introduction

Preserving is a way of making sure that fresh foods can be kept for longer, making sure they do not go to waste. This was very important in years past, when the vegetable plot outside the back door provided the food that you ate each day. Preserving was a way to keep food on the table in the winter months. Today, when food is grown in huge quantities and imported year-round, and commercial preserves are easy to buy, there is less reason to make preserves, yet many of us still love to do it. There is something very special about cooking a batch of raspberry jam from fruit picked from the garden, or making something delicious from foraged blackberries and apples.

I was brought up in a family where we used to come home to pots of green tomato chutney gracing the table, and it was very comforting to see a larder full of homemade marmalades and other delicacies. Today, knowing where all your food has come from is a rarity. It has made me appreciate simply cooked vegetables and how to make the most of what you have. The freshness and flavour that goes with homemade is not something you can buy.

I have always found it therapeutic and enjoyable to find ways to use up fruit or vegetables through pickling and preserving. I now have my own children and they are always keen to get involved in chopping onions and making jams – it is quite a family affair when we are all in the kitchen! Chutney has not quite got the thumbs up yet, but they love homemade raspberry jam, particularly in a jam tart.

If you tend an allotment or have a vegetable patch, it does focus your mind on making an effort to use up your precious produce; a glut of tomatoes or courgettes can very quickly go to waste. We are fairly obsessed in my family with waste, so we preserve, where we can, any food that we grow and we have chickens who eat our leftovers. I do confess to having no tasty answers to using a huge cabbage glut though, which I think many of us picklers find challenging!

There are so many fruits and berries you can eat for free if you know where to look. Foraging from the trees and hedgerows during the summer and autumn can be a great way to get out and be active. Children can learn about the seasons and what grows when, and it's a great way to spend time together as a family. Start with fruits that grow abundantly near you, as it will be inexpensive to experiment. Sloes in the autumn

steeped in a bottle of gin makes the most delicious sloe gin to be drunk on a winter's day. For bought produce your local market or pick-your-own is the most affordable way to get a good deal on a large quantity of fruit, and you can pick the best of the bunch.

Whatever you decide to make, give yourself plenty of time. Get your jars prepared before you start to cook, as jellies and jams can set quite quickly and you want your jars ready to fill. Once you have tried a few recipes, you will get to understand what sets well and what doesn't. You can start to be inventive with your ingredients and work with what you have to hand. The pot is your oyster and anything goes.

What is Preserving?

Storing food for a long time needs a little bit of science. There are lots of methods you can use, such as curing, salting, drying and covering with a layer of fat, as well as cooking using sugar, vinegar and alcohol. All these methods help to prevent your preserves from spoiling and to last as long as you want them to.

All raw foods contain enzymes that help to sustain life as well as breaking them down, causing food to discolour and rot over time. Preserving halts the enzymes developing any further, keeping the food at its best. Preserving also works by drying up or killing off micro-organisms (for example, moulds, yeasts and bacteria) that might enter your preserves and spoil your hard work. A high concentration of sugar, vinegar or alcohol along with cooking at a high temperature will prevent the growth of micro-organisms.

Mould is not actually harmful to eat but it tastes and looks unpleasant and can indicate that bacteria are present, which can cause food poisoning. Yeasts cause foods to ferment, which is not wanted in your jam but can be a good thing in cider and breadmaking. In jam or other preserves, fermenting could mean that unwanted bacteria are present. Hygiene plays an important part in keeping your preserves bacteria free, which is why sterilizing your jars and lids is so important (see page 14). There are many ways to preserve fruit and vegetables as well as meat and fish:

Jams

A combination of fruit and sugar cooked until they set to a soft, spreading consistency. The fruits used must contain pectin (see page 15–16), which helps them to set. If the fruit is low in pectin, such as strawberries, it can be combined with a fruit high in pectin, such as lemon, to help the jam to set.

Conserves

Similar to jams but are usually a softer set. The best fruits to use are soft fruits such as strawberries and raspberries; these are usually left in sugar for 24 hours before cooking, to extract their juice. Some conserves are made with dried fruits, such as mincemeats.

Marmalades

Again, similar to jams but are made from citrus fruits, peel and sugar. The peel must be cooked for a long time so that it softens before the sugar is added.

Jellies

Made from the juice of fruit, which is allowed to drip, then the sugar is added and the jelly cooked until set. Jellies can be served in the same way as jam, but they are most often served with meat, poultry and cheese.

Curds

Made from fruit juice, sugar and eggs. Eggs are added to thicken the mixture to a rich, soft spreading consistency. Curds are considered a preserve, as traditionally they were made when there was a glut of fruit, but they are not preserves in the true sense, as they will keep only for a few weeks in a refrigerator.

Butters

Made from fruits and sugar that are cooked slowly for a long time until their consistency resembles soft butter. They are used in a similar way to jam but do not keep as long so should only be made in small quantities.

Cheeses

Similar to butters but are very thick and can be potted into jars or small moulds and turned out to serve with cold meat and cheeses. They keep much longer than butters and improve with storage.

Fruits in alcohol

Many fruits lend themselves to this preservation method, particularly stone fruits such as cherries and apricots. Like vinegar, alcohol prevents the growth of bacteria. These preserves, like conserves, are delicious served as a dessert or with cheese. Whole fruits, such as clementines, can also be conserved in sugar syrup (see pages 18 and 100).

Chutneys

A vinegar preserve made from one or a mixture of vegetables and fruit. Chutneys are cooked for a long time in vinegar, sugar, spices and salt until the mixture is reduced to a pulp, the consistency of a thick sauce. Chutneys need to mature as they improve with time.

Relishes

Similar to chutneys and the two are often confused. To clear up the confusion, relish contains more clearly defined vegetables and fruit as they are chopped into larger pieces and the mixture is cooked for less time. Relish recipes often focus on one key ingredient.

Pickles

Preserve whole or sliced vegetables or fruits by cooking in spiced, sweetened vinegar. They may also be salted before being cooked.

Sauces

Blended or puréed preserves, made in a similar way, and with similar ingredients, to vinegar preserves, not dissimilar to chutney mixtures. Usually made from one predominant fruit or vegetable. They are puréed after cooking so that they are smooth, such as the popular tomato ketchup.

Candying

A sugar preserve method that works by soaking fruits in sugar syrup so that they are saturated with sugar. Crystallized fruit is then coated in sugar and left to dry.

Curing

A method of preserving meat, fish, vegetables and nuts using salt and drying. Salting draws out the water from the enzymes, which stops their growth and prevents the food going rancid. Drying closes the pores on the surface of the food so that it doesn't become exposed to air and harmful micro-organisms. Many cured foods are then s moked, which doesn't actually preserve the food but flavours or cooks it.

Drying

Used to preserve herbs, and some fruits and vegetables, drying works well for apples, pears, plums, chillies, onions and mushrooms. If this method of preserving interests you, you may wish to buy an electric food dehydrator to speed up the process.

Under fat

A method of preserving meat, fish and cheese under a layer of fat to seal it from the air, moisture and micro-organisms. These are short-term preserves and need to be stored in the refrigerator.

Ingredients

Choosing the best fruit and vegetables and the correct sugar and vinegar for your recipe will ensure you get the results you want. Finding excellent fresh produce has never been easier. You can forage, grow your own, shop at farm shops and farmers' markets, visit pick-your-own and swap home-grown produce at neighbourhood swap schemes. Preserve-making is so popular that you can find unusual sugars and vinegars and other ingredients in most supermarkets, and readily online. It is easy to get started!

Choosing fruit and vegetables

Aim to preserve fruit and vegetables when they are at their peak. This can vary according to the weather, and you can find your preserve-making time varies each year. You may find that if it has been a very dry year, you need to add more liquid to your recipe, and vice versa. Your produce should be ripe but not overripe as it may contain more water than you expect, which may prevent the preserve setting. Many fruits freeze well, which means you can buy or harvest produce at its best and make your preserves when convenient for you. Seville oranges are perfect for freezing, which saves you having to make a whole year's supply of marmalade in one go. Choose large, heavy citrus fruits for marmalades, as they are the juiciest. Some fruits, such as sloes, benefit from freezing. The best fruits and vegetables to freeze are those with a low water content or a hard skin, such as citrus fruit and apples. Strawberries and raspberries do not freeze well, but can still be used to make delicious preserves; a perfect way to use a bumper crop. A little of the pectin in the fruit is lost during freezing but this can be solved by adding an additional 10 per cent of fruit to the quantity stated in the recipe. When preparing your produce, discard any bruised or damaged parts as this will affect the quality and flavour of your preserve.

Alcohol

To act as a preservative, the alcohol that you use must be 80 per cent proof to inhibit the growth of micro-organisms. Spirits such as brandy, gin, kirsch, rum and whisky are all suitable. Wines, fortified wines and cider can also be used but they must be combined with sugar or heat-treated to work as a preservative.

Fat

Butter, goose and duck fat are the traditional fats used to seal out oxygen from preserves and so prevent micro-organisms entering. A fine layer of clarified fat is often used to cover pâtés and terrines. Oils are used too, particularly for preserving Mediterranean vegetables and cheeses, such as goats' cheese. As the flavour of oil will impact on the preserve, use extra virgin olive oil; if you have any left in the jar after eating, the flavoured oil will make a delicious salad dressing, or you can use it to drizzle over grilled meat or fish.

Salt

Another important ingredient in preserves, salt inhibits the growth of micro-organisms. Ordinary cooking salt is suitable to use, especially as it is often needed in large quantities. Avoid table salt as this often contains anti-caking agents. For seasoning, you may prefer to use a sea salt, which can add its own distinctive flavour.

Spices and flavourings

If you make a lot of preserves you will soon have quite a collection of spices. They are important to give the final preserve its flavour and can be used whole or ground. Whole spices can be tied in a square of muslin/cheesecloth and removed after cooking if you don't want them in the finished preserve. Ground spices are useful for chutneys and relishes, as they make a clear preserve cloudy. Pickling spices are often used to flavour the vinegar in pickles, and blends can be bought ready-prepared. They vary in flavour so read the ingredients list. See page 137 to make your own.

Sugar

White granulated sugar is suitable for most preserves. Golden granulated sugar, caster/superfine, lump/rock, Demerara, light and soft brown sugars can also be used but are more expensive; they are useful if you want to achieve a certain flavour or colour. Preserving sugar is more expensive than granulated and is not necessary, but it does reduce the amount of scum that develops during cooking. Jam/gelling sugar contains added pectin and should be used with fruits that are low in pectin, such as strawberries. Most recipes will still require a mix of jam sugar and granulated sugar so the set is not too firm. Icing/powdered sugar is not suitable for use in preserving.

Vinegar

The colour, flavour and acetic acid content of vinegars varies widely so aim to use the correct one for each recipe. The acetic acid content should be at least 5 per cent for preserve-making, so that micro-organisms can't survive. Vinegar colour is no indication of its acid content so you need to read the label.

Malt vinegar is made from fermented barley, and the dark variety is coloured by added caramel. White malt vinegar has been distilled and is a good choice for light-coloured pickles. It is sometimes described on the label as distilled white vinegar or distilled malt vinegar.

Red and white wine vinegars come from grapes and have a more delicate flavour than malt vinegar, as does cider vinegar, which is sweeter. It goes particularly well with apple chutneys. Balsamic vinegar is expensive by comparison to other vinegars but adds a distinct, delicious flavour along with its rich, dark colour. Sherry vinegar can also be very useful for colour and flavour. The vinegar used for pickles is usually spiced and you can either buy it or make your own.

SPICED VINEGAR

Pour 1l/34fl oz/4 cups distilled white vinegar or white wine vinegar into a saucepan and add your choice of spices (see page 137). Slowly bring to the boil but do not allow it to bubble. Pour into a bowl or bottles, cover and leave to infuse for 2 hours. Strain the mixture before use.

Alternatively, you can add the spices to the vinegar without heating and leave to infuse for 1–2 months to intensify the flavour. Pour into clean, dry bottles and seal with airtight, vinegar-proof lids. Label and store in a cool, dry, dark place.

Equipment

I am not a great one for adding equipment to my kitchen cupboard, and you can make a lot of the recipes in this book without lots of specialist equipment. If you have a decent heavy-based saucepan you can get going, and improvise along the way. If you want to make lots of preserves, one or two purchases will make your life easier. A sugar or jam thermometer is probably the most useful implement to buy, as it can help you to find setting points accurately.

Bowl

You will need at least one large bowl for straining the liquid for a jelly and for brining vegetables for pickles. A selection of smaller-size bowls are useful for holding your prepared ingredients.

Chopping board

You will need a large chopping board for preparing fruit and vegetables. I particularly like flexible cutting mats, as you can lift the prepared food and scoop it straight into the preserving pan. They are lightweight and dishwasher-safe, too, for easy, effective cleaning.

Funnel

Useful for filling jars to prevent the preserve from spilling down the sides of the jar. You need to sterilize it each time you use it. Alternatively, you can use a heatproof jug/pitcher to pour preserves into the jars.

Jars and bottles

Use either jars and bottles with a screw-top lid or wide-necked jars with glass or metal lids, secured by clips. They don't have to be new but it is essential that they are sterilized before use. I would, however, recommend that you use new lids and rubber rings, as secondhand ones could be damaged and could result in a poor seal. Lids can be bought in packs of various sizes from kitchen shops and online suppliers. If the preserve contains a high percentage of vinegar then you will need to use a vinegar-proof lid, which is lined with white plastic, or you can use a Kilner jar with a rubber seal. Kilner jars are useful for potting larger fruits as they have a wide neck.

Jelly bag

This is used to strain the pulp into a bowl when making jellies. It has handles, which can be suspended from an upturned stool or chair. If you don't have one, you can improvise by using a double thickness of material, such as a dish towel, J-cloth or piece of muslin/cheesecloth.

Knife

A large, sharp knife is an essential piece of equipment for preparing the fruit and vegetables. Sharpen it regularly.

Lemon squeezer

An essential, inexpensive piece of equipment for many marmalade and jam recipes.

Measuring jug/cup, scales and spoons

Measuring your ingredients accurately is important when making preserves, so these are the few essential items that you should buy if you haven't got them.

Muslin

Small squares of muslin/cheesecloth are needed for tying pips and spices in when making marmalade or flavouring pickles. You can buy small muslin bags for this purpose, too. You can also improvise by using a J-cloth or medical gauze. The pips and spices are then easy to remove after cooking.

Preserving pan

A preserving pan is designed to hold a large quantity of ingredients so your preserve can boil rapidly without it boiling over. It has a thick, heavy base so your preserve won't stick to the bottom, graduated sides to ensure that any liquid evaporates quickly, and handles and a spout to make jarring easier.

If you already own a large steel saucepan you can get started, but make sure your ingredients only come halfway up the sides. You may need to cook smaller batches, and add longer simmering and boiling times, as evaporation will be slower.

If you want to buy a preserving pan, choose stainless steel, as it conducts the heat evenly and quickly. Aluminium also conducts the heat well and is less expensive, but choose a heavy-gauged pan, as lightweight pans can dent and bow. Copper and brass pans should not be used for making chutneys, relishes and pickles as the vinegar will react with the pan and

taint the flavour of the preserve. You can use them for fruit preserves but make sure you remove the preserve quickly to prevent acid damage.

Sieve/strainer

Used to purée fruit or make a smooth sauce, this can be used as an alternative to a food processor, especially if you need to discard the seeds. Use a heatproof nylon sieve rather than a metal one, as the acid in the fruit can react with the metal.

Slotted spoon

Useful for scooping stones/pits out of a preserve, and skimming the scum off jams, jellies and marmalades.

Sugar thermometer

This is very useful for finding an accurate setting point for your jams and jellies and it ensures that they reach the correct temperature to destroy any harmful bugs. If you don't have one, you can still test a preserve's setting point by following the Saucer or Flake Test (see page 21).

Wooden spoon (long-handle)

Good for stirring hot preserves so that your hand doesn't get too close. Some metals can discolour the preserves, so wood is the sensible choice.

Specialist equipment

If you want to get really serious about preserving you may want to invest in a digital pH meter which checks the acidity of your preserve, and a refractometer, which measures sugar concentration. Both can help you achieve exactly the set you want and help to determine the preserve's shelf life. This can help you maintain the same consistency in a product, particularly if you plan to sell your preserves.

Sterilizing Bottles & Jars

The importance of sterilizing cannot be emphasized enough; it is essential so that your preserves do not deteriorate during storage. Always sterilize an extra bottle or jar in case it is needed. Remove any labels if you are reusing bottles or jars, and wash all in very hot, soapy water. Then follow one of the following methods to sterilize your bottles or jars.

In the oven

Do not dry the washed bottles or jars but put them on a baking sheet, about 5cm/2in apart, and put in the oven. Turn on the heat to 180°C/350°F/Gas 4 and, once the oven has reached this temperature, leave the bottles or jars in the oven for 20 minutes to ensure they are completely sterilized. Most preserves will be hot when potted so it makes sense to keep the bottles or jars in the oven until needed; reduce the temperature slightly. Wear protective oven gloves when handling the hot bottles and jars.

In a saucepan

Put the washed bottles or jars in a large saucepan, ensuring they do not touch each other. Fill the pan with enough water to cover by 2.5cm/1in, slowly bring to the boil and boil for 10 minutes. Carefully remove the bottles or jars from the pan and put on a baking sheet. Put in the oven at 180°C/350°F/Gas 4 and leave in the oven for 20 minutes until dry.

In the dishwasher

Put the washed bottles or jars in the dishwasher and then run the hottest cycle. If the bottles or jars need cleaning first, you will need to run the dishwasher twice. Fill the bottles or jars while they are still hot.

Sterilizing lids

Put the lids in a saucepan of water, bring to the boil and boil for 10 minutes. Make sure they are dry before use to avoid condensation forming. An alternative method is to fill the hot sterilized bottles or jars with the hot preserve, screw on the lids and then turn the bottles or jars upside down for 1 minute. Wear protective oven gloves or cover the bottle or jar with a dish towel when you do this to avoid burning yourself. This effectively sterilizes the insides of the lids and means that you don't need to use wax paper or film discs to cover the preserve before putting the lids on.

Sterilizing equipment

It is important that all your cooking equipment is scrupulously clean, too, to prevent bacteria passing into your preserves. Like bottles and jars, make sure that all pans, bowls, jugs, funnels and utensils are washed in very hot, soapy water and rinsed well, or run through the hottest dishwasher cycle just before use, even if they were washed well last time you used them.

EMMA'S TIP Use the sterilized jars while they are still hot so that they do not crack when filled with the hot preserve.

Making Sweet Preserves

Jams, jellies, marmalades, butters and cheeses are all made following the same basic tried-and-tested methods, which produce their correct setting consistency, and it is their high concentration of sugar that preserves them.

All sweet preserves need pectin and acid to make them set. Fruits rich in pectin are usually rich in acid, too. If a fruit or vegetable has a low content of pectin or acid, it can be combined with a fruit with a high content to help it set. Lemon juice is often used to add extra acid where needed. As a guide, add 2 tablespoons lemon juice for every 2kg/4lb 8oz fruit. You can also buy liquid or powdered pectin, which does not add a particular flavour so is very versatile.

Sweet preserves need a lot of sugar; the exact amount depends on the pectin content of the fruit, so always use the amount given in the recipes. It might be tempting to add less, but it will result in a preserve that won't set and it will also not keep well.

All sweet preserves are made by preparing the fruit, adding water and simmering until the mixture is soft and reduced. When you add the sugar and any extra pectin varies for each recipe.

The cooking time for each recipe will depend on how hard or soft the fruit is. Don't try to speed up the cooking process, as it is during this time that the natural pectin and acid in the fruit are released.

When making jellies, the fruit is cooked to a pulp and then allowed to drip through a jelly bag to extract the fruit's juices. Whether you use a traditional jelly bag or you improvise, your bag should be scalded in boiling water before you use it so that the juices drip through it and are not absorbed by the bag. It's very tempting to squeeze the bag or prod the pulp but try to resist, as it will produce a cloudy jelly. The general rule for jellies is to add 500g/1lb 2oz/2¼ cups sugar to every 600ml/21fl oz/scant 2½ cups of juice extract.

Butter and cheese preserves are made to have a firm set. The general rule is to add 350g/12oz/scant 1⅔ cups sugar to every 600ml/21fl oz/scant 2½ cups of purée when making a butter, and 500g/1lb 2oz/2¼ cups sugar to every 600ml/21fl oz/scant 2½ cups of purée when making a cheese. The sugar is added to the fruit once soft, otherwise it hardens the fruit and any peel, and will not soften further during cooking.

How much sugar?

Fruit with a high natural pectin content needs more sugar than fruit with low pectin. As a rough guide this is the amount of sugar you will need:

- 1kg/2lb 4oz fruit with a high pectin content needs up to 1.25kg/2lb 12oz/5⅔ cups granulated sugar

- 1kg/2lb 4oz fruit with a medium pectin content needs up to 1kg/2lb 4oz/4½ cups granulated sugar

- 1kg/2lb 4oz fruit with a low pectin content needs about 800g/1lb 12oz/3⅔ cups granulated sugar

Fruit and vegetable pectin content

Natural pectin content does vary from year to year and during the season due to a fruit's quality and different environmental conditions. It is also higher just before ripening. To test the pectin content of a fruit, add 1 teaspoon cooked fruit juice to 1 tablespoon methylated spirits, gin or whisky. If it forms a firm clot it is high in pectin; if it forms small clots it is medium; if it remains liquid it is low in pectin.

High	Medium	Low
Blackcurrants	Apricots	Bananas
Cooking apples	Bilberries	Blackberries (late)
Crab apples	Blackberries (early)	Blueberries
Cranberries	Eating apples	Carrots
Damsons	Greengages	Cherries
Gooseberries	Loganberries	Courgettes/ zucchini
Grapefruits	Mulberries	Elderberries
Grapes	Raspberries	Figs
Japonicas	Sloes	Marrows
Lemons		Medlar
Limes		Melons
Oranges		Nectarines
Plums (most varieties)		Peaches
Quinces		Pears
Redcurrants		Pineapple
White currants		Pumpkin
		Rhubarb
		Rosehips
		Strawberries

The key to all sweet preserves is making sure the sugar dissolves properly before you boil. You can warm the sugar beforehand in the oven at a low temperature so it dissolves quickly when in the fruit. Do not stir too much during the boiling time, as it can cool the preserve. The boiling time will vary depending on the fruit used.

When testing for a set, take the pan off the heat so that the preserve doesn't cook unnecessarily for too long. Setting point is usually 105°C/221°F (see page 21).

Some recipes ask you to remove 'scum' from the surface of your sweet preserve; scum is the bubbles caused by rapid boiling and is removed to help with the final appearance of the preserve. Adding a little butter helps to remove the scum but it is not essential.

Preserves containing whole fruits or peel should be left to cool for about 15 minutes before jarring to prevent the fruit or peel from rising in the jars.

Candied and crystallized fruits

These are other sweet preserves that rely on sugar to preserve them but are made by a different method. They are made by steeping the fruits in a sugar syrup over a period of time so that they soak up the sugar to a high concentration. Crystallized fruits are candied fruits that are then finely coated in a layer of sugar.

EMMA'S TIP The recipes give the quantities each preserve makes but, in the case of jellies, this is a guide only. It will depend on how ripe the fruit was and how long it was left to drip, as these factors affect how much juice is obtained.

Making Savoury Preserves

Chutneys, relishes, pickles and sauces have been made for generations as a way to preserve precious fruits and vegetables, and because they taste delicious. The basic method stays the same and uses vinegar, salt and/or sugar as the preservative. Cooks have experimented over the years with different ingredients to bring their preserves to life.

Chutneys and relishes are made in a similar way; the main differences are the preparation of the fruit and vegetables and their cooking time, which affect their final appearance. The ingredients for a relish are usually chopped into small pieces, while those for chutney are roughly chopped. Chutneys are cooked for a long time, reducing the fruits and vegetables to a thick, pulpy mixture, whereas relishes are cooked for a shorter time, resulting in a chunkier texture.

Unlike jam-making, you can use very ripe fruits and vegetables for savoury preserves but do remove any damaged or bruised pieces. It is worth spending time carefully preparing fruit and vegetables for a relish as your slicing skills will be visible in the final preserve. You need to cook chutneys and relishes very slowly in a preserving pan or large saucepan, stirring from time to time to prevent them from sticking to the bottom of the pan. This is especially important near the end of cooking. Use a stainless steel pan, as the vinegar in the preserve will react with copper or brass pans.

Pickles are usually made from a single fruit or vegetable and can be raw or cooked. Your produce should be firm and fresh so that its texture and flavour are kept during storage. Many pickles are salted or 'brined' first, either by dry salting where they are layered in salt (produce such as cucumbers that contain a lot of water use this method), or by wet salting, where they are soaked in a solution of salt and water. This draws out moisture and helps to retain colour and crispness. After brining, rinse well and pat dry; wet vegetables will dilute the vinegar and the pickle is more likely to turn mouldy.

Pickle texture

Cold vinegar is added to make crisp pickles and hot vinegar added to make soft pickles. Some, such as Piccalilli, are cooked in a sauce, but the key is to retain the shape and texture of each vegetable in the pickle. Packing your jars too tightly can bruise the pickle; make sure all the ingredients are submerged in the liquid.

Sauces, such as tomato ketchup, are puréed to give a smooth, pouring consistency. You can purée using a food processor or push the mixture through a nylon sieve/strainer to make it smooth (metal sieves can taint a sauce's flavour).

Storage and maturing

All preserves that contain vinegar should be covered with a clip-top glass lid or lids that have a vinegar-proof lining; metal lids will rust in direct contact with vinegar. Almost all chutneys, relishes and pickles should be allowed to mature for at least a month before eating, as they really do improve with age. They can be stored for at least a year. Pickled cabbage is an exception; it can't be stored for more than 3 weeks, as it loses its crispness. Sauces are best eaten within 3 months, or you can bottle them to prolong their storage life (see page 23). You can also store them in the freezer.

Making Bottled Fruits & Drinks

Bottled fruits, in either syrup or alcohol, make delicious desserts, and it is an excellent way to preserve whole or sliced fruits. Freezing has tended to replace the need to bottle fruits, but a bottle or two can be a treat and make attractive gifts.

Choose fresh, perfect-quality fruit for bottling, as presentation is part of the appeal. Choose attractive bottles and jars with wide necks so you can get the fruit in easily. Take time arranging the fruit in the bottle or jar so that they look attractive. It is traditional, for example, to arrange slices around the outside. Use the handle of a wooden spoon to move the fruit into position and pack tightly but without squashing or damaging them; the fruit are then less likely to rise in the jar.

If you plan to use liqueur or a spirit to cover the fruit it must have at least 40 per cent alcohol to act as a preservative. Test that the flavour is compatible with the fruit used. Brandy complements most fruits. Kirsch, of course, works with cherries, but it is also delicious with raspberries and pineapple. Wines, fortified wines, sherry and cider can be used to bottle fruit but need to be combined with sugar to act as a preservative.

Syrups and cordials

Homemade fruit syrups and cordials are full of flavour and have more adult appeal than many commercial soft drinks. Most fruit syrups and cordials are made from soft berry fruits, such as blackcurrant, and they need to be just ripe. The juices are extracted from the fruit, usually by being left to soak in water overnight, then strained, cooked with sugar the following day, and strained again before being bottled. Soft fruit drinks do not have a long storage life but, stored in plastic bottles, they can be kept in the freezer. Allow a head-space at the top of the bottles to allow for the liquid to expand.

Fruit liqueurs such as Limoncello (see page 120) are made by infusing a spirit with fruit, sometimes with the addition of sugar to sweeten, and left in a warm place for several months. The infused liquid is transferred into sterilized bottles and can keep for many years. If you like, the fruits can be served separately as an alcoholic dessert. Gin was traditionally flavoured with sloes and damsons, rum works very well with plums, and vodka and blackcurrants are also a great match.

Mincemeats

Brandy, rum and sherry all work well in mincemeat. The dried fruits are preserved in both sugar and alcohol and it is particularly important that the fruits are well submerged.

EMMA'S TIP The recipes indicate the size and number of jars that you need, but when packing fruits in jars it is difficult to be specific, as it depends on the size of the fruits and how tightly you pack them. It is advisable to have an extra jar ready just in case it is needed.

Making Cured, Dried & Potted Preserves

Curing and drying works by removing moisture so micro-organisms cannot grow. Curing used to be a very popular way of preserving meat but is less often used now due to freezing. Traditional methods such as potting remain popular as they enhance flavour and texture.

Cured preserves

Many people enjoy the flavour curing brings to food and some meats can be dried in the home (see page 221) although it does need a lot of care. Many cured foods, such as salmon, are also smoked, which dries the food further and adds flavour. If you want to smoke food, you can buy or make a smoker to give food a delicious smoky flavour, but it won't actually preserve it. For suggestions on the type of salt to use, see page 10. Very fresh, cold meat and fish should be used for curing, not frozen, as freezing makes food cells expand and absorb more salt than is needed.

Dried preserves

Drying fruits and vegetables is less complicated, although some foods are more suitable than others. Apples, apricots, pears, plums, onions, mushrooms and herbs can all be dried successfully in the home, either in an oven or a warm airing cupboard. The temperature must be low enough to dry, rather than bake the food, as otherwise it will shrivel. Ventilation is needed and the longer the period over which the food is dried, the better for success. You can buy domestic dehydrators, which can be useful if you have a large supply of produce to dry. Choose fresh, perfect-quality fruit and vegetables that are just ripe and don't have any bruises or blemishes. Once dried, it is important to store the food away from any moisture to preserve it, as the food may absorb water again and start to rehydrate.

Potted preserves

Potting preserves foods under a seal of fat. This excludes moisture and air from getting into them and therefore any harmful micro-organisms. Potted foods, such as pâtés and terrines, are 'short-term' preserves as they must be kept in the refrigerator and cannot be stored for a long time. Once the seal of fat is broken, the preserve should be eaten within a week. Like curing foods, meat or fish to be potted is usually layered with salt to remove as much moisture as possible, and then cooked for a long time until tender. The most suitable meats to use are rich, fatty meats such as duck. The fat you use to form a seal can be goose, duck or pork fat, or you can use clarified butter, or oils such as extra virgin or virgin olive, sunflower or rapeseed/canola.

Preserves prepared commercially in oil are acidified to prevent micro-organisms from growing and can be stored for several months at room temperature, but when prepared in the home they should be considered a 'short-term' preserve and stored in the refrigerator. Herbs, spices and garlic that are packed in bottles of oil for display in the kitchen should be regarded as a pretty decoration and not as a preserve, as it is unlikely that they have been prepared for consumption.

After opening, make sure the preserve is always covered in oil. The leftover oil can be strained through a sieve and stored in the refrigerator for a few weeks. It can then be used in salad dressings and marinades, drizzled over warm vegetables, brushed over grilled fish or meat or used to fry steaks and chicken pieces.

Is it Cooked?

You can cook a batch of plum jam or apple chutney one year and have a completely different experience the next. Every variety of fruit and vegetable differs in how long it takes to cook, and this changes from year to year, too. If you are new to preserve-making it can take a while to work out when 'setting-point' has arrived, or when your preserve is at the right consistency for potting or jarring. There are a number of ways to test whether your preserve is cooked.

The natural sugar content, moisture and acidity of a fruit or vegetable are affected by the weather and growing conditions, so one year your tomatoes may need longer to cook, or more sugar adding. Different varieties of a fruit or vegetable vary too: apple varieties, for example, vary hugely in their natural sweetness. Later in the season, fruit and vegetables may be softer and contain more water, or be starchier in texture. This natural variance can affect your set, so you do need to be able to work out if your preserve has cooked, rather than rely completely on a recipe cooking time.

The cold saucer method (see opposite) for testing setting points is a useful way for you to gain confidence. You can touch and feel when a preserve is set. I often use three saucers or ramekins when trying a new recipe, which I place in the freezer in advance, so I can test more than once during the cooking time. Once you have made a few preserves you will feel confident about what a preserve looks like when it has reached setting point.

Jams, marmalades and jellies

Once a jam, marmalade or jelly is at boiling point, continue with a rolling boil until it thickens. A rolling boil has a steady bubbling across the whole surface. At this stage you need to test that the 'setting point' has

been reached and the preserve is cooked. These times vary so start testing for setting early in order to avoid overcooking the preserve. You should also take the pan off the heat while testing to avoid overcooking, which will affect the flavour and can prevent setting. If your preserve hasn't yet reached setting point, return it to the heat and boil for a further 5 minutes, then repeat the test, removing from the heat again while you do so.

Chutneys and relishes

To test that a chutney or relish has reached the correct consistency and is cooked, there should be no excess liquid on the surface, and the mixture should be thick. If you drag a wooden spoon through the mixture to form a channel you should be able to see the bottom of the pan. If the channel immediately fills with liquid it is not cooked. If the channel remains visible for 2 seconds the preserve is cooked. Retest every few minutes if necessary.

Curds, butters and cheeses

To test that a curd has reached the correct consistency and is cooked, dip in a wooden spoon; the curd should be creamy and thick enough to coat the back of the spoon. This will happen well before it reaches a boil, which should not be allowed, as boiling

Saucer test

Flake test

will curdle and spoil the mixture. A butter is cooked when it is thick enough to spread like jam. A cheese is cooked when a wooden spoon, drawn across the bottom of the pan, leaves a clear channel through it.

Testing for setting point

Your preserve is cooked when it reaches 'setting point' and it becomes heavy and glossy. You are then ready to pour it into your sterilized jars.

SAUCER TEST If you don't have a thermometer, put a saucer or ramekin dish in the freezer before you start cooking. When you think your preserve has reached setting point, take the saucer or ramekin dish out of the freezer and put a teaspoon of the preserve on it. Leave for 2–3 minutes and, when cool, push it with your finger. If the preserve wrinkles and holds its

shape, setting point has been reached. If not, return to the heat for further cooking.

FLAKE TEST Using a wooden spoon, lift a little of the preserve out of the pan. Twirl the spoon around, leave the preserve to cool a little and then let it drop back into the pan. If it does not run off the spoon, but drops of the preserve run together along the edge of the spoon and form flakes that fall off sharply, setting point has been reached.

THERMOMETER TEST Using a sugar thermometer is the most reliable way to test a setting point. When the preserve reaches 105°C/221°F, setting point has been reached and you should stop cooking. Preserves that have a high pectin content will reach setting point at a few degrees lower.

> **EMMA'S TIP** When you are ready to test if your preserve is cooked, take the pan off the heat so there is no danger of overcooking. You can always put it back on the heat again if it needs longer to cook.

Potting, Covering, Bottling & Storing

When your preserve is cooked and you are ready to pot it, a few tips on the best way to put it in your sterilized bottles or jars, cover it and store it, will help to keep it at its best.

Potting

In most cases it is best to fill a hot jar with a hot preserve. What you shouldn't do is fill a hot jar with a cold preserve or a cold jar with a hot preserve, as the jar might crack. Stand the jars on a wooden board, as they might crack if on a cold surface when the hot preserve is poured in. Using a funnel, fill the jar to within 1cm/½in of the top, and before sealing, tap the jar lightly on a hard surface or run a sterilized spoon through the contents of the jar to release any trapped air pockets that might harbour micro-organisms.

Covering

Cover the jars immediately to prevent bacteria in the air getting in. Screw-top sterilized lids or clip-top lids with a sealing ring provide an effective seal, but you can also opt for waxed discs with a cellophane round 'lid'. Dampen one side of the cellophane round with a clean, damp cloth and place over the hot jar, dampened side uppermost. Pull tightly to seal and secure with an elastic band. When the preserve has cooled, the cover will be tight. It is traditional to cover the cellophane with paper or fabric, tied with string

Recommended storage times

Eat your preserves before these times to make sure they taste at their best. After this time, your preserves may start to deteriorate:

Alcoholic preserves	1 month (or 3 years if bottled)
Chutneys, relishes and pickles	1–2 years
Curds	2 weeks
Fruit butters	9 months
Fruit cheeses	1 year
Fruit conserves	1 month (or 1 year if bottled)
Fruit liqueurs	2–3 years
Jams and jellies	1 year
Marmalades	1–2 years
Mincemeats	1 year
Sauces	3 months to 1 year

or an elastic band. This works well to deter bacteria and looks attractive if you are giving it as a gift. There is no need to use a waxed disc with a lid, unless there is vinegar in your preserve.

Wipe the jars clean with a damp cloth, but, in the case of jams, marmalades and jellies, do not move the preserve until it is set as it may displace pieces of fruit in the preserve or cause uneven cooling, which again, can lead to fruit settling or sinking.

Label the preserve with its contents and with the date; you may think that you will remember what is inside the jar but it can be easy to forget. You could add a list of ingredients, too.

Bottling

If potting an uncooked preserve, you can pasteurize it using the 'bottling' method so that it lasts longer. Jars covered with cellophane rounds are not suitable for this method. There are two ways to do this: the first is to put the filled jars on a rack in a large saucepan, making sure that they do not touch each other. Pour in enough water to come halfway up the sides of the jars. Bring the water to the boil, turn the heat down slightly, cover and simmer for 1 hour.

The second way is to pasteurize the filled jars in a vegetable steamer for 1 hour. Whichever method you use, keep an eye on the water level and top up with more water when needed.

Storing

Store preserves in a cool, dry, dark place. Kept in the correct conditions, most preserves can be stored for over a year. Traditionally, most preserves were eaten within a year to make room for next year's preserves. Most chutneys, relishes and pickles should be stored for at least 1 month but preferably for 2–3 months before eating to allow their flavour to mature and mellow (cabbage is an exception, see page 17). Once opened, store the preserve in the refrigerator.

Use your own judgement when it comes to deciding if your preserve has deteriorated. If it smells unpleasant, then it probably won't be good to eat! It was once thought that, if mould had developed on the top, the mould could be removed and the remaining preserve was safe to eat. This is now considered a potential health risk and the preserve should be thrown away.

EMMA'S TIP A good-looking label can make all the difference, especially if you are giving the preserve as a gift. You can buy labels ready-made, or if you are feeling creative, buy label paper with a peel-off backing and make your own. Simple designs are often the most effective; a drawing of the fruits or vegetables that are in the preserve can look lovely. If you prefer, a coloured line, in the same colour as the preserve around the edge of the label to create a frame can look attractive. Choose waterproof markers if hand-writing labels so the information does not deteriorate over time.

Alternatively, tie a cardboard label around the neck of the bottle or jar with string or ribbon. Attractive labels look appealing and professional and reflect the work you have put in.

Troubleshooting

Having spent many hours stirring pots of preserves, I felt it would be useful to include a troubleshooting guide so that if something should go wrong during your cooking, you might be able to rescue it. In most cases things only go wrong for me when I have been interrupted or am in a hurry; if you can avoid this then that will be a great start.

Quick fixes

Preserving is reasonably easy if you follow the basic rules, but every now and again something can go wrong. These are the problems you might encounter while you are making preserves, and I give you tips so that you can rectify them there and then.

UNSET JAM, JELLY OR MARMALADE

If your preserve has not set after cooling, it may be due to undercooking. In this case you can pour it back into the saucepan and continue to cook until setting point is reached.

FRUIT OR PEEL FLOATING TO THE SURFACE

If the fruit or peel rises to the surface of the pan after it has been cooked, leave the preserve to cool for about 15 minutes. This especially applies to jams and marmalades containing large pieces of fruit and thick-cut peel. This gives the fruit time to absorb the sugar, which makes it heavy so that it is suspended in the syrup rather than floating to the surface. Stir well to distribute the fruit or peel and then pour into jars. Conserved fruits in syrup that rise in the jar indicate that they were not packed correctly; they should be tightly packed in a jar of the correct size.

CURDS NOT SMOOTH

The curd has been cooked at too high a temperature and has caused the eggs to curdle. The problem may be rectified by removing it from the heat very quickly and whisking with a balloon whisk until smooth. This may work but will depend how far the curdling has gone. Curdling can also occur if you do not continue to stir the egg during cooking. This causes bits of egg to coagulate in the mix and they will look white. The only remedy for this is to sieve the curd before potting.

Fruit or peel floating to the surface

BUTTERS AND CHEESES TOO SOFT

They have not been cooked long enough (see Is it Cooked? page 20). The problem can be solved by further cooking.

MINCEMEAT FERMENTING IN JAR

This can be caused by incorrect storage conditions or inaccurate weighing of ingredients such as too little sugar or lemon juice, too much apple or not enough alcohol. If in doubt, smell and taste the mincemeat. You may be able to rectify fermented mincemeat if you catch it early enough by transferring the mincemeat to a saucepan, boiling for 1–2 minutes and adding a splash of brandy or more dried fruit. Pack into newly warmed, sterilized jars, taking care to remove any air bubbles, cover immediately and leave to cool. Store in the refrigerator or freeze in bags until you need it. Don't just use it for Christmas, as it can be added to lots of different puddings and cakes.

MINCEMEAT DRYING OUT

This is probably caused by storing the mincemeat in too warm a place or not having enough liquid to start with; the fruit soaks up more liquid over time. When you want to use the mincemeat, stir in a little alcohol such as sherry or brandy, or the alcohol used in the original recipe, to add moisture.

LIQUID COLLECTING AT THE TOP OF CHUTNEY OR RELISH

This is caused because the preserve was not cooked long enough for sufficient liquid to evaporate. It can be rectified by further cooking. Return it to the pan, bring to the boil and cook until the excess liquid has evaporated. Spoon into warmed, sterilized jars and seal.

DARK-COLOURED PICKLES

This can occur if you haven't used enough preserving liquid to completely cover the fruit or vegetables. They might look unattractive but there is no cause for alarm and they are safe to eat.

Tips for next time

If a problem has occurred once you have made your preserve, it may just mean that it looks unattractive and doesn't necessarily mean that it has to be thrown away. All is, therefore, not lost, and on a positive note, you will learn from experience and all will be well next time you make it.

PRESERVE WON'T SET

Lack of pectin is the usual cause if your preserve won't set. This could be due to the type of fruit used or if the fruit is overripe, in which case the pectin may have deteriorated. Another reason is not cooking the preserve for long enough; it needs time for the pectin to be released and the water to evaporate. Further cooking should rectify this.

Using incorrect proportions of fruit and sugar and overcooking after adding the sugar are other reasons the preserve has failed to set, but this cannot be rectified.

If the jam hasn't set after potting, return it to the pan, add the juice of 1 small lemon and return to the boil. Test for a set and, when setting point has been reached, ladle into warmed, sterilized jars and seal.

MOULD ON THE SURFACE

This can be caused by not sterilizing the jars correctly; for example, if the jars are damp or cold. Not potting the preserve while it is still hot and not covering it immediately can also cause the development of mould, along with not filling jars to the top. Storing a preserve in a very warm or damp place can lead to mould, too. When making a pickle, always wash the fruit or vegetables well because they are not cooked and any micro-organisms remaining may lead to mould. It is not advised to eat a preserve that has mould on it.

PRESERVE HAS CRYSTALLIZED

Not allowing the sugar to dissolve completely before bringing the preserve to the boil, or using too much sugar, can cause crystallization. It cannot be remedied but the preserve is still safe to eat. As it will taste sweet and have a crunchy texture it is ideally best used in cooking. If crystals have formed on top of the preserve after it has been opened, they are caused by evaporation of liquid.

SHRINKING FROM SIDES OF JAR

This is due to evaporation and is caused by not making the preserve airtight when covering. Over-boiling during cooking can also cause the preserve to shrink from the sides of the jar, as can storing the jar in a too warm, damp, or light place. The best solution is to eat the preserve as soon as possible.

CHUTNEY, RELISH, JAM, MARMALADE OR JELLY HAS A BURNT FLAVOUR

This occurs when the preserve is not stirred enough during cooking and some has stuck to the bottom of the pan, causing it to burn. There is no remedy for this, and having done this plenty of times in the past, my only advice is to give yourself lots of time to cook and never walk away from a boiling pan!

DULL COLOUR IN PRESERVES

Dullness is caused either by cooking the jam for too long before adding the sugar, or boiling it for too long once it has been added. It's fine to eat but just not sparkling and attractive.

FADING COLOUR IN PRESERVES

Fading especially applies to red fruits such as strawberries and raspberries. Incorrect storage is the problem, and the fading has been caused by storing the preserve in too light or warm a place, or storing it for too long. It may still be all right to eat, so taste a little to be sure.

DARKENING AT THE TOP OF JAR

This can occur if the preserve is not sealed and indicates that air has got in, causing oxidation. This can occur naturally over time with light-coloured preserves

Bubbles in jam, jellies and marmalades

and chutneys and is perfectly safe. Give it a quick stir before serving to improve the appearance. This problem can also occur if the preserve has been incorrectly stored in too warm or light a place. If there are other signs of deterioration, such as mould, then do not eat, but if you are sure it is just due to storage, then it is safe to eat.

BUBBLES IN JAM, JELLIES AND MARMALADES

This can be an indication that fermentation has occurred during storage; the jam may also smell gassy when you remove the lid. It can be due to the jars not being sterilized or sealed correctly. It can also be caused by too little sugar in the finished product, undercooking of the jam, or inaccurate weighing of the ingredients. This problem may have been apparent earlier as the preserve would not have set correctly. If the jam has fermented it should not be eaten.

If there is no indication of fermentation, bubbles may just be caught in the scum that often forms during cooking. This preserve is safe to eat but just does not look as good as it could. Swirling 1 teaspoon of butter into the jam at the end of cooking can help to reduce and disperse scum. You can also just skim off the scum with a metal spoon before potting.

WEEPING JAMS, JELLIES AND MARMALADES

Caused because the preserve was stored in too warm a place or the storage temperature fluctuated. The preserve can still be eaten but will be soft.

TOUGH PEEL IN MARMALADE

The peel wasn't cooked for long enough before adding the sugar, which then further hardens the peel. Unfortunately, the problem can't be rectified.

JELLY TOO STIFF

The jelly contained too much pectin because the fruit was under-ripe or it was overcooked. Another time use ripe fruit and test for a set earlier.

JELLY LOOKS CLOUDY

You were tempted to poke or squeeze the bag while the liquid was dripping and this has caused it to go cloudy. It cannot be rectified but the jelly will still be edible. Leave the jelly to drip at its own pace next time. Jelly can also look cloudy if you used under-ripe fruit, which can release its starch and turn the jelly cloudy.

CHUTNEY, RELISH OR PICKLE HAS A METALLIC FLAVOUR

The preserve has been cooked in a brass or copper preserving pan, which imparts a metallic flavour due to the reaction of the pan with the vinegar. In future, use an aluminium or stainless steel pan.

SOFT OR TOUGH PICKLES

Soft pickles can be caused by using vinegar with low acidity or not using enough salt, whereas too much salting can cause tough pickles. Soft pickles can also occur if you decide to pasteurize your pickles in a hot water bath or you keep them for a long time before eating (over 12 months). Always use a vinegar with a 5–7 per cent acid content and measure the salt accurately. Storing in a warm place will also cause pickles to soften.

Jams & Marmalades

Raspberry Jam

Serve this classic jam spread on toast or scones for a delicious taste of summer, or in Bakewell and jam tarts. You could also serve a spoonful with vanilla ice cream or hot custard for a quick dessert. This recipe also works well with loganberries.

MAKES ABOUT: 1.8KG/4LB **PREPARATION TIME:** 20 MINUTES **COOKING TIME:** 20 MINUTES

1kg/2lb 4oz/8 cups raspberries
juice of 1 lemon
1kg/2lb 4oz/4½ cups granulated sugar
1 tsp butter

1 Put the raspberries and lemon juice in a preserving pan and slowly raise the heat until the juices start to run. Simmer gently for 5 minutes to allow the raspberries to soften slightly.

2 If you prefer a seedless jam, push the raspberries through a fine sieve and return to the pan. Discard the seeds in the sieve.

3 Add the sugar to the pan and stir until completely dissolved. Bring to the boil and boil rapidly for about 10 minutes until setting point is reached. Test for a set either with a sugar thermometer (it should read 105°C/221°F) or put a teaspoon of the jam onto a cold saucer and leave to cool for a few minutes. If it wrinkles when you push it with your finger, then it is ready to use.

4 Meanwhile, sterilize enough jars in the oven so that they are ready to use (see page 14).

5 Remove the pan from the heat. Swirl in the butter. If any scum remains, skim with a slotted spoon.

6 Ladle the jam into the warmed, sterilized jars. Cover immediately with waxed discs and dampened cellophane rounds or lids. Label and store in a cool, dry, dark place. Refrigerate after opening.

Morello Cherry Jam

Dark red morello cherries (or 'sour' cherries) are excellent for cooking as they have a concentrated cherry flavour. They are not easy to find sold fresh, but this recipe also works well with sweet dessert cherries.

MAKES ABOUT: 1.7KG/3LB 12OZ   **PREPARATION TIME:** 20 MINUTES   **COOKING TIME:** 45 MINUTES

3 lemons
1kg/2lb 4oz/5 cups morello cherries, pitted
1kg/2lb 4oz/4½ cups granulated sugar
1 tsp butter

1 Using a sharp knife or potato peeler, pare the zest from the lemons and then slice the zest very finely. Halve the lemons and squeeze out the juice and pips. Tie the pips in a piece of muslin/cheesecloth.

2 Put the lemon zest, lemon juice, muslin bag and 1.2l/40fl oz/4¾ cups water in a preserving pan and slowly bring to the boil.

3 Reduce the heat and simmer for about 10 minutes until the liquid is reduced by two-thirds and the zest is soft.

4 Remove the muslin bag from the pan, squeezing it well and allowing the juices to run back into the pan. Discard the bag.

5 Add the cherries and simmer for about 20 minutes until soft.

6 Add the sugar to the pan and stir until the sugar has completely dissolved. Bring to the boil and boil rapidly for 10–15 minutes until setting point is reached. Test for a set either with a sugar thermometer (it should read 105°C/221°F) or put a teaspoon of the jam onto a cold saucer and leave to cool for a few minutes. If it wrinkles when you push it with your finger, then it is ready to use.

7 Meanwhile, sterilize enough jars in the oven so that they are ready to use (see page 14).

8 Remove the pan from the heat. Swirl in the butter. If any scum remains, skim with a slotted spoon.

9 Ladle the jam into the warmed, sterilized jars and cover immediately with a waxed disc and a dampened cellophane round or a lid. Label and store in a cool, dry, dark place. Refrigerate after opening.

EMMA'S TIP It would be worth investing in a cherry stoner/pitter for this recipe as it really does save time. Alternatively, you can cook the cherries with their stones in and remove them from the pan with a slotted spoon as they float to the surface, before adding the sugar.

The Best Strawberry Jam

The flavour of summer, packed into a jar. Strawberries lack pectin, which means this jam needs jam sugar to set. Serve spread on scones with clotted cream or crème fraîche, use to sandwich a Victoria sponge cake or indulge in a spoonful straight from the jar.

MAKES ABOUT: 1.7KG/3LB 12OZ **PREPARATION TIME:** 25 MINUTES, PLUS 15 MINUTES COOLING
COOKING TIME: 15 MINUTES

1kg/2lb 4oz small strawberries, or
    large strawberries, halved
juice of 2 lemons
550g/1lb 4oz/2½ cups granulated sugar
400g/14oz/heaped 1¾ cups jam/gelling sugar
    with added pectin
1 tsp butter

1 Put the strawberries and lemon juice in a preserving pan and slowly raise the heat until the juices start to run. Simmer gently for 5 minutes to allow the strawberries to soften slightly.

2 Add the granulated and jam sugar to the pan and stir until completely dissolved. Bring to the boil and boil rapidly for 6–8 minutes until setting point is reached. Test for a set either with a sugar thermometer (it should read 105°C/221°F) or put a teaspoon of the jam onto a cold saucer and leave to cool for a few minutes. If it wrinkles when you push it with your finger, then it is ready to use.

3 Meanwhile, sterilize enough jars in the oven so that they are ready to use (see page 14).

4 Remove the pan from the heat. Swirl in the butter. If any scum remains, skim with a slotted spoon. Leave the jam to cool for 15 minutes (this will help to prevent the fruit from rising in the jars).

5 Ladle the jam into the warmed, sterilized jars. Cover immediately with a waxed disc and a dampened cellophane round or a lid. Label and store in a cool, dry, dark place. Refrigerate after opening.

> **EMMA'S TIP** Using whole small strawberries makes a beautiful jam, which is perfect for spooning onto scones, but you can use large strawberries sliced in half, too. You might like to invest in a strawberry huller as it really does make the strawberry preparation simpler.

Blackcurrant Jam

This jam, with its intense, fruity flavour, is delicious served spread on bread or toast. You could also try a spoonful with pancakes, drop scones, rice pudding or yogurt.

MAKES ABOUT: 2.5KG/5LB 8OZ **PREPARATION TIME:** 15 MINUTES, PLUS 15 MINUTES COOLING
COOKING TIME: 1 HOUR

1kg/2lb 4oz/8⅓ cups blackcurrants, stripped
1.5kg/3lb 5oz/heaped 6¾ cups
    granulated sugar
1 tsp butter

1 Put the blackcurrants and 875ml/30fl oz/ 3½ cups water in a preserving pan and slowly bring to the boil.

2 Reduce the heat and simmer gently for about 45 minutes until the blackcurrants are very soft but have not disintegrated into a pulp, and the liquid is well reduced. Stir from time to time to prevent the mixture from sticking to the bottom of the pan.

3 Add the sugar to the pan and stir until completely dissolved. Bring to the boil and boil rapidly for about 10 minutes, or until setting point is reached. Test for a set either with a sugar thermometer (it should read 105°C/221°F) or put a teaspoon of the jam onto a cold saucer and leave to cool for a few minutes. If it wrinkles when you push it with your finger, then it is ready to use.

4 Meanwhile, sterilize enough jars in the oven so that they are ready to use (see page 14).

5 Take the pan off the heat. Swirl in the butter. If any scum remains, skim with a slotted spoon. Allow the jam to cool for 15 minutes (this will help to prevent the fruit from rising in the jars).

6 Ladle the jam into the warmed, sterilized jars and cover immediately with a waxed disc and a dampened cellophane round or a lid. Label and store in a cool, dry, dark place. Refrigerate after opening.

Strawberry & Rhubarb Jam

Strawberries and rhubarb are in season at the same time and make a happy marriage. The strawberries sweeten the tart rhubarb and it makes a good jam to serve as a breakfast spread or spooned on top of yogurt.

MAKES ABOUT: 2KG/4LB 8OZ **PREPARATION TIME:** 20 MINUTES, PLUS 15 MINUTES COOLING
COOKING TIME: 40 MINUTES

1kg/2lb 4oz small strawberries,
   or large strawberries, halved
1kg/2lb 4oz rhubarb, sliced into
   1cm/½in pieces
1.5kg/3lb 5oz/heaped 6¾ cups
   granulated sugar
juice of 2 lemons
juice of 1 orange
1 tsp butter

1 Put the strawberries and rhubarb in a preserving pan and heat gently until the juices start to run.

2 Slowly bring to the boil, then reduce the heat and simmer gently for about 20 minutes until the fruits are soft and the liquid is well reduced. Stir from time to time to prevent the mixture from sticking to the bottom of the pan.

3 Add the sugar to the pan and stir until completely dissolved. Add the lemon and orange juice, bring to the boil and boil rapidly for about 15 minutes, or until setting point is reached. Test for a set either with a sugar thermometer (it should read 105°C/221°F) or put a teaspoon of the jam onto a cold saucer and leave to cool for a few minutes. If it wrinkles when you push it with your finger, then it is ready to use.

4 Meanwhile, sterilize enough jars in the oven so that they are ready to use (see page 14).

5 Take the pan off the heat. Swirl in the butter. If any scum remains, skim with a slotted spoon. Leave the jam to cool for 15 minutes (this will help to prevent the fruit from rising in the jars).

6 Ladle the jam into the warmed, sterilized jars and cover immediately with a waxed disc and a dampened cellophane round or a lid. Label and store in a cool, dry, dark place. Refrigerate after opening.

EMMA'S TIP Vanilla complements both strawberries and rhubarb and you need just a hint to flavour the jam. Split a vanilla pod/bean in half, scrape out the seeds, and add both the seeds and pod to the fruit at the beginning of cooking. Remove the pod before cooling.

High Dumpsideary Jam

It is thought that this jam gets its unusual name from a Mrs Dumpsideary. Finding there was nothing left to put on her toast, Mr Dumpsideary solves the problem by making her a jam from windfall autumn fruit and spices that he had in the cupboard. It is a very useful recipe if you have a glut of plums, apples and pears.

MAKES ABOUT: 3.8KG/8LB 4OZ **PREPARATION TIME:** 45 MINUTES **COOKING TIME:** 45 MINUTES

500g/1lb 2oz plums, roughly chopped,
    and stones/pits reserved
grated zest and juice of 1 lemon
15g/½oz fresh ginger, bruised
2 cloves
1 cinnamon stick
500g/1lb 2oz cooking apples, peeled,
    cored and roughly chopped
500g/1lb 2oz firm, under-ripe pears,
    peeled, cored and roughly chopped
25g/1oz/scant ¼ cup raisins
1.3kg/3lb/scant 6 cups granulated sugar
1 tsp butter

1 Tie the plum stones, lemon zest, ginger, cloves and cinnamon in a piece of muslin/cheesecloth.

2 Put the muslin bag and all the ingredients, except the sugar and butter, in a preserving pan. Add 150ml/5fl oz/scant ⅔ cup water and slowly bring to the boil. Reduce the heat and simmer gently for 20–30 minutes, depending on the ripeness of the fruit, until they are soft. Stir from time to time to prevent the mixture from sticking to the bottom of the pan.

3 Remove the muslin bag from the pan, squeezing it well and allowing the juice to run back into the pan. Discard the bag.

4 Add the sugar to the pan and stir until completely dissolved. Bring to the boil and boil rapidly for about 15 minutes or until setting point is reached. Test for a set either with a sugar thermometer (it should read 105°C/221°F) or put a teaspoon of the jam onto a cold saucer and leave to cool for a few minutes. If it wrinkles when you push it with your finger, then it is ready to use.

5 Meanwhile, sterilize enough jars in the oven so that they are ready to use (see page 14).

6 Remove the pan from the heat. Swirl in the butter. If any scum remains, skim with a slotted spoon.

7 Ladle the jam into the warmed, sterilized jars. Cover immediately with a waxed disc and a dampened cellophane round or a lid. Label and store in a cool, dry, dark place. Refrigerate after opening.

Spiced Victoria Plum Jam

You can use whichever variety of plums you have to make this jam. At Bay Tree we use Victoria plums, but golden or damson plums will be delicious, too, although of course the colour will change. Just make sure your plums are very ripe.

MAKES ABOUT: 1.7KG/3LB 12OZ **PREPARATION TIME:** 40 MINUTES, PLUS 15 MINUTES COOLING
COOKING TIME: 45 MINUTES

1kg/2lb 4oz Victoria plums, halved and
    stones/pits reserved
2 cinnamon sticks, halved
4 whole cloves
juice of 1 lemon
1kg/2lb 4oz/4½ cups granulated sugar
1 tsp butter

1 Tie the plum stones, cinnamon sticks and cloves in a piece of muslin/cheesecloth.

2 Put the plums, muslin bag and lemon juice in a preserving pan. Add 300ml/10½fl oz/scant 1¼ cups water and slowly bring to the boil. Reduce the heat and simmer gently for 20–30 minutes, depending on the ripeness of the plums, until the fruit and skins are soft. Stir from time to time to prevent the mixture from sticking to the bottom of the pan.

3 Remove the muslin bag from the pan, squeezing it well and allowing the juice to run back into the pan. Discard the bag.

4 Add the sugar to the pan and stir until the sugar has completely dissolved. Bring to the boil and boil rapidly for 10–15 minutes until setting point is reached. If the plums are rising to the surface, cook for a further 2–4 minutes to allow the plums to absorb more of the sugar. Test for a set either with a sugar thermometer (it should read 105°C/221°F) or put a teaspoon of the jam onto a cold saucer and leave to cool for a few minutes. If it wrinkles when you push it with your finger, then it is ready to use.

5 Meanwhile, sterilize enough jars in the oven so that they are ready to use (see page 14).

6 Remove the pan from the heat. Swirl in the butter. If any scum remains, skim with a slotted spoon. Leave the jam to cool for 15 minutes (this will help to prevent the fruit from rising in the jars).

7 Ladle the jam into the warmed, sterilized jars and cover immediately with a waxed disc and a dampened cellophane round or a lid. Label and store in a cool, dry, dark place. Refrigerate after opening.

Wild Apricot & Almond Jam

Using hard, dried Hunza apricots that come from wild apricot trees in the Hunza valley, Pakistan, creates a jam with an intense, toffee-like flavour. You need to soak the apricots beforehand overnight, but otherwise this is a very simple recipe. This is the jam to serve with warmed croissants in the morning.

MAKES ABOUT: 2.25KG/5LB **PREPARATION TIME:** 20 MINUTES, PLUS 12 HOURS SOAKING
COOKING TIME: 1 HOUR

450g/1lb/2½ cups dried Hunza apricots
juice of 1 lemon
1.3kg/3lb/scant 6 cups granulated sugar
55g/2oz/⅓ cup blanched almonds, halved
1 tsp butter

1 Put the apricots in a large bowl. Add 1.75l/60fl oz/6⅔ cups water and leave to soak for 12 hours.

2 The next day, put the soaked apricots and the water in a preserving pan. Add the lemon juice and slowly bring to the boil. Reduce the heat and simmer gently for about 30 minutes until the apricots are soft. Stir from time to time to prevent the mixture from sticking to the bottom of the pan.

3 Add the sugar and almonds to the pan and stir until the sugar has completely dissolved. Bring to the boil and boil rapidly for 20–25 minutes until setting point is reached. Test for a set either with a sugar thermometer (it should read 105°C/221°F) or put a teaspoon of the jam onto a cold saucer and leave to cool for a few minutes. If it wrinkles when you push it with your finger, then it is ready to use.

4 Meanwhile, sterilize enough jars in the oven so that they are ready to use (see page 14).

5 Remove the pan from the heat. Swirl in the butter. If any scum remains, skim with a slotted spoon.

6 Ladle the jam into the warmed, sterilized jars and cover immediately with a waxed disc and a dampened cellophane round or a lid. Label and store in a cool, dry, dark place. Refrigerate after opening.

EMMA'S TIP If you can't find Hunza apricots then substitute with organic dried apricots. Pre-soaked, plump 'ready-to-eat' apricots won't have the same rich flavour.

Billy Banana Jam

The Fruit Orchard Kids were jam jars, cookie jars and statues that were made in the United States in 1942. There were six in total, the others being Stella Strawberry, Charlie Cherry, Lee Lemon, Albert Apple and Penny Pineapple. We've used the name for this delicious jam. Spread on fresh bread or combine it with peanut butter in a sandwich.

MAKES ABOUT: 1KG/2LB 4OZ **PREPARATION TIME:** 15 MINUTES **COOKING TIME:** 20 MINUTES

1kg/2lb 4oz ripe bananas, peeled
680g/1lb 8oz/heaped 3 cups granulated sugar
juice of 1 lemon

1 Put the bananas in a food processor and blend to make a rough purée.

2 Put the banana purée in a preserving pan and add the sugar and lemon juice. Slowly bring to the boil, stirring all the time to prevent the mixture from sticking to the bottom of the pan. Reduce the heat and continue stirring for 10–15 minutes until the mixture is thick. The jam is ready when a wooden spoon drawn across the base of the pan reveals it cleanly. (There is no need to test for a set.)

3 Meanwhile, sterilize enough jars in the oven so that they are ready to use (see page 14).

4 Ladle the jam into the warmed, sterilized jars. Cover immediately with a waxed disc and a dampened cellophane round or a lid. Label and store in a cool, dry, dark place. Refrigerate after opening.

EMMA'S TIP This is a good way to use up very ripe bananas (under-ripe bananas will be too starchy for this recipe). You can spread it on bread, but it is also delicious used as a topping on ice cream, pancakes and waffles. You could try spicing it up by adding ½ tsp ground cloves, 1 tsp ground cinnamon, 1 tsp cardamom or 1 tsp vanilla extract. You can also add 50g/1¾oz/½ cup chopped walnuts or 70g/2½oz/½ cup currants at the end of cooking. For a caramel flavour you could use soft light brown sugar instead of granulated sugar.

Spiced Carrot Jam

Vegetable jams are popular in the Middle East and lend themselves to the addition of spices. This is a delicious way to preserve an abundant crop of carrots. Serve it on crusty bread or a bagel with cream cheese.

MAKES ABOUT: 1.7KG/3LB 12OZ **PREPARATION TIME:** 30 MINUTES **COOKING TIME:** 55 MINUTES

1kg/2lb 4oz carrots, grated
grated zest and juice of 1 lemon
grated zest and juice of 2 oranges
1 tsp ground cinnamon
½ tsp ground cloves
¼ tsp grated nutmeg
1kg/2lb 4oz/4½ cups granulated sugar
1 tsp butter

1   Put the carrots, lemon and orange zests and juices, cinnamon, cloves and nutmeg in a preserving pan. Add 875ml/30fl oz/3½ cups water and slowly bring to the boil. Reduce the heat and simmer for about 20 minutes until the carrots are tender and the liquid is well reduced. Stir from time to time to prevent the mixture from sticking to the bottom of the pan.

2   Add the sugar to the pan and stir until the sugar has completely dissolved. Bring to the boil and boil rapidly for about 30 minutes or until setting point is reached. Test for a set either with a sugar thermometer (it should read 105°C/221°F) or put a teaspoon of the jam onto a cold saucer and leave to cool for a few minutes. If it wrinkles when you push it with your finger, then it is ready to use.

3   Meanwhile, sterilize enough jars in the oven so that they are ready to use (see page 14).

4   Remove the pan from the heat and pack the carrot well into the warmed, sterilized jars, topping up with the liquid. Cover immediately with a waxed disc and a dampened cellophane round or a lid. Label and store in a cool, dry, dark place. Refrigerate after opening.

Butternut Squash, Ginger & Citrus Jam

This vibrant, orange jam tastes rich and zesty and has a soft, spreading consistency. It isn't too sweet and tastes good spread on toast as well as muffins and pancakes. It can even be used in a chicken or turkey sandwich in the same way as you would use chutney.

MAKES ABOUT: 1.8KG/4LB **PREPARATION TIME:** 35 MINUTES **COOKING TIME:** 55 MINUTES

1.5kg/3lb 5oz butternut squash, peeled
   and deseeded
100g/3½oz fresh ginger, peeled and finely
   sliced into small pieces
grated zest and juice of 3 lemons
grated zest and juice of 4 oranges
grated zest and juice of 1 lime
1 tsp ground ginger
½ tsp ground cinnamon
800g/1lb 12oz/3⅔ cups granulated sugar

1 Grate the butternut squash, either by hand or in a food processor.

2 Put all the ingredients, except the sugar, in a preserving pan. Add 1l/34fl oz/4 cups water and slowly bring to the boil.

3 Reduce the heat and simmer for about 20 minutes until the squash is soft. Stir from time to time to prevent the mixture from sticking to the bottom of the pan.

4 Add the sugar to the pan and stir until completely dissolved. Bring to the boil and boil rapidly for about 30 minutes until no excess liquid remains and the mixture is thick. Stir from time to time. The jam is ready when a wooden spoon drawn across the base of the pan reveals it cleanly. (There is no need to test for a set.)

5 Meanwhile, sterilize enough jars in the oven so that they are ready to use (see page 14).

6 Ladle the jam into the warmed, sterilized jars. Cover immediately with a waxed disc and a dampened cellophane round or a lid. Label and store in a cool, dry, dark place. Refrigerate after opening.

EMMA'S TIP Pumpkins also work well in this recipe and, if you are making lanterns for Halloween, it is a great way of using up the flesh. The jam would be lovely spread on cupcakes or cookies, and you could add a ghost or spider decoration, too!

Sweet Tomato Chilli Jam

This fiery, flecked red jam is really a relish and it goes with a range of dishes. Try it with cold meats, bread and cheese or barbecued burgers. You can also serve it alongside fishcakes to add a little gentle heat.

MAKES ABOUT: 1.4KG/3LB 2OZ **PREPARATION TIME:** 35 MINUTES, PLUS 15 MINUTES COOLING
COOKING TIME: 25 MINUTES

1kg/2lb 4oz tomatoes
juice of 2 lemons
2 tsp dried chilli flakes
¼ tsp sea salt
1kg/2lb 4oz/4½ cups granulated sugar

1 With a sharp knife, cut a cross in the top of each tomato. Put the tomatoes in a heatproof bowl and cover with boiling water. Leave to stand for 2–3 minutes, then drain. Peel off and discard the skins. Roughly chop the flesh.

2 Put the tomatoes, lemon juice, chilli flakes and sea salt in a preserving pan and bring to the boil. Reduce the heat and simmer for 5 minutes until the tomatoes are softened.

3 Add the sugar to the pan and stir until the sugar has completely dissolved. Bring to the boil and boil rapidly for 10–15 minutes until setting point is reached. Test for a set either with a sugar thermometer (it should read 105°C/221°F) or put a teaspoon of the jam onto a cold saucer and leave to cool for a few minutes. If it wrinkles when you push it with your finger, then it is ready to use.

4 Meanwhile, sterilize enough jars in the oven so that they are ready to use (see page 14).

5 Remove the pan from the heat and leave the jam to cool for 15 minutes (this helps to prevent the tomatoes from rising in the jars).

6 Ladle the jam into the warmed, sterilized jars and cover immediately with a waxed disc and a dampened cellophane round or a lid. Label and store in a cool, dry, dark place. Refrigerate after opening.

Rose Petal Jam

Known as gulkand in India, where it is very popular, rose petal jam is made by leaving the petals in full sunshine. This is a version that doesn't rely on such demands. It is, however, a jam to make if you have an abundance of red roses. Serve at a summer afternoon tea on sweet biscuits or meringues, or use as a cake filling with the addition of whipped cream and fresh strawberries or raspberries. You could scatter the tablecloth with extra rose petals!

MAKES ABOUT: 600G/1LB 5OZ **PREPARATION TIME:** 30 MINUTES, PLUS 12 HOURS STANDING
COOKING TIME: 50 MINUTES

225g/8oz freshly picked, dark red,
   heavily-scented rose blooms
500g/1lb 2oz/2¼ cups granulated sugar
juice of 2 lemons
culinary rose extract (optional)

1 Remove the petals from the rose blooms and snip off and discard the white bases. Cut the petals into small pieces and put in a bowl.

2 Add 250g/9oz/scant 1¼ cups of the sugar to the petals. Cover and leave to stand at room temperature for 12 hours or overnight to extract the rose flavour and darken the petals.

3 The next day, put the lemon juice, 1.2l/40fl oz/4¾ cups water and the remaining sugar in a heavy-based saucepan. Gently heat the mixture, stirring until the sugar has dissolved, but do not let it boil.

4 Stir in the rose petal mixture and simmer gently for 30 minutes. Slowly bring to the boil and boil rapidly for about 15 minutes until thick. (There is no need to test for a set.)

5 Meanwhile, sterilize enough jars in the oven so that they are ready to use (see page 14).

6 Remove the pan from the heat and remove any scum with a slotted spoon. Taste (be careful as it will be hot), and if the jam doesn't have a distinct rose flavour, add a few drops of rose extract, or to taste.

7 Ladle the jam into the warmed, sterilized jars. Cover immediately with a waxed disc and a dampened cellophane round or a lid. Label and store in a cool, dry, dark place. Refrigerate after opening.

EMMA'S TIP You will need about 16 rose blooms to make up the weight required for this recipe.

Traditional Marmalade

The season for Seville oranges is short, so make a batch of this classic marmalade in late winter or freeze the fruit and make it when convenient. Seville oranges are best for marmalade as they produce a good flavour and contain more pectin than sweet oranges. Marmalades made with sweet oranges will have a cloudier appearance.

MAKES ABOUT: 5KG/11LB **PREPARATION TIME:** 45 MINUTES, PLUS 20 MINUTES COOLING
COOKING TIME: 2 HOURS 20 MINUTES

1.5kg/3lb 5oz Seville oranges
juice of 2 lemons
3kg/6lb 8oz/13⅔ cups granulated sugar

1 Halve the oranges and squeeze out the juice and pips. Tie the pips, and any extra membrane that has come away during squeezing, in a piece of muslin/cheesecloth.

2 Either by hand or using the shredding attachment of a food processor, slice the orange peel, with its pith, into thin, medium or thick shreds, according to your preference.

3 Put the orange juice and peel, lemon juice, muslin bag and 3.5l/122fl oz/13½ cups water in a preserving pan and slowly bring to the boil. Reduce the heat and simmer gently for about 2 hours until the peel is very soft and the liquid reduced by about half.

4 Remove the muslin bag from the pan and leave to cool for 5 minutes before squeezing it well and allowing the juices to run back into the pan. Discard the bag.

5 Add the sugar to the pan and stir until completely dissolved. Bring to the boil and boil rapidly for about 15 minutes, or until setting point is reached. Test for a set either with a sugar thermometer (it should read 105°C/221°F) or put a teaspoon of the marmalade onto a cold saucer and leave to cool for a few minutes. If it wrinkles when you push it with your finger, then it is ready to use.

6 Meanwhile, sterilize enough jars in the oven so that they are ready to use (see page 14).

7 Remove the pan from the heat and skim with a slotted spoon to remove any scum. Leave to cool for 15 minutes (this will help to prevent the peel from rising in the jars).

8 Ladle the marmalade into the warmed, sterilized jars and cover immediately with a waxed disc and a dampened cellophane round or a lid. Label and store in a cool, dry, dark place. Refrigerate after opening.

Lime & Lemon Shred Marmalade

The combination of these two citrus fruits produces a refreshing, zesty marmalade. Use it to spread on toast or to flavour homemade breakfast muffins.

MAKES ABOUT: 2.25KG/5LB **PREPARATION TIME:** 45 MINUTES, PLUS 20 MINUTES COOLING
COOKING TIME: 1 HOUR 45 MINUTES

500g/1lb 2oz limes
250g/9oz lemons
1.5kg/3lb 5oz/heaped 6¾ cups
    granulated sugar

1 Halve the limes and lemons and squeeze out the juice and pips. Tie the pips, and any extra membrane that has come away during squeezing, in a piece of muslin/cheesecloth.

2 Either by hand or using the shredding attachment of a food processor, thinly slice the lime and lemon peel, with its pith, into shreds.

3 Put the lime and lemon juice and peel, muslin bag and 1.75l/60fl oz/6⅔ cups water in a preserving pan and slowly bring to the boil. Reduce the heat and simmer gently for about 1½ hours until the peel is very soft and the liquid reduced by half.

4 Remove the muslin bag from the pan and leave to cool for 5 minutes before squeezing it well and allowing the juices to run back into the pan. Discard the bag.

5 Add the sugar to the pan and stir until the sugar is completely dissolved. Bring to the boil and boil rapidly for about 10 minutes or until setting point is reached. Test for a set either with a sugar thermometer (it should read 105°C/221°F) or put a teaspoon of the marmalade onto a cold saucer and leave to cool for a few minutes. If it wrinkles when you push it with your finger, then it is ready to use.

6 Meanwhile, sterilize enough jars in the oven so that they are ready to use (see page 14).

7 Remove the pan from the heat and skim with a slotted spoon to remove any scum. Leave to cool for 15 minutes (this will help to prevent the peel from rising in the jars).

8 Ladle the marmalade into the warmed, sterilized jars and cover immediately with a waxed disc and a dampened cellophane round or a lid. Label and store in a cool, dry, dark place. Refrigerate after opening.

Orange, Lemon & Ginger Marmalade

Ginger adds a warming kick to marmalade. Delicious on toast, this marmalade is also good stirred into natural yogurt or used in baked puddings.

MAKES ABOUT: 1.9KG/4LB 3OZ **PREPARATION TIME:** 45 MINUTES, PLUS 15 MINUTES COOLING
COOKING TIME: 1¾–2¼ HOURS

500g/1lb 2oz oranges
375g/13oz lemons
115g/4oz fresh ginger, peeled and finely
    sliced into small pieces
1 tbsp ginger paste
1kg/2lb 4oz/4½ cups granulated sugar

1 Halve the oranges and lemons and squeeze out the juice and pips. Tie the pips, and any extra membrane that has come away during squeezing, in a piece of muslin/cheesecloth.

2 By hand or using the shredding attachment of a food processor, thinly slice the orange and lemon peel, with its pith, into thin, medium or thick shreds, according to your preference.

3 Put the orange and lemon juice and peel, the muslin bag and 2.4l/84fl oz/9½ cups water in a preserving pan and slowly bring to the boil. Reduce the heat and simmer gently for 1½–2 hours until the peel is soft and the liquid reduced by about half.

4 Remove the muslin bag from the pan and leave to cool for 5 minutes before squeezing it well and allowing the juice to run back into the pan. Discard the bag.

5 Add the ginger, ginger paste and sugar to the pan and stir until the sugar is completely dissolved. Bring to the boil and boil rapidly for about 15 minutes, or until setting point is reached. Test for a set either with a sugar thermometer (it should read 105°C/221°F) or put a teaspoon of the marmalade onto a cold saucer and leave to cool for a few minutes. If it wrinkles when you push it with your finger, then it is ready to use.

6 Meanwhile, sterilize enough jars in the oven so that they are ready to use (see page 14).

7 Remove the pan from the heat and skim with a slotted spoon to remove any scum. Leave to cool for 15 minutes (this will help to prevent the shreds from rising in the jars).

8 Ladle the marmalade into the warmed, sterilized jars and cover immediately with a waxed disc and a dampened cellophane round or a lid. Label and store in a cool, dry, dark place. Refrigerate after opening.

Lemon & Lavender Marmalade

Lavender's strong flavour complements that of sharp citrus fruits, making it the perfect pairing with lemons. Serve this marmalade with toast or muffins.

MAKES ABOUT: 2.25KG/5LB **PREPARATION TIME:** 45 MINUTES, PLUS 15 MINUTES COOLING
COOKING TIME: 1¾–2¼ HOURS

750g/1lb 10oz lemons
2 tsp dried or ¾ tsp fresh culinary
   lavender flowers
1.5kg/3lb 5oz/heaped 6¾ cups
   granulated sugar
½ tsp lavender extract

1 Halve the lemons and squeeze out the juice and pips. Tie the pips, and any extra membrane that has come away during squeezing, in a piece of muslin/cheesecloth.

2 Either by hand or using the shredding attachment of a food processor, thinly slice the lemon peel, with its pith, into shreds.

3 Put the lemon juice and peel, muslin bag and 1.75l/60fl oz/6⅔ cups water in a preserving pan and slowly bring to the boil. Reduce the heat and simmer gently for 1½–2 hours until the peel is really soft and the liquid reduced by about half.

4 Remove the muslin bag from the pan and leave to cool for 5 minutes before squeezing it well and allowing the juices to run back into the pan. Discard the bag.

5 Add the lavender flowers and sugar to the pan and stir until the sugar has completely dissolved. Bring to the boil and boil rapidly for about 15 minutes or until setting point is reached. Test for a set either with a sugar thermometer (it should read 105°C/221°F) or put a teaspoon of the marmalade onto a cold saucer and leave to cool for a few minutes. If it wrinkles when you push it with your finger, then it is ready to use.

EMMA'S TIP You can buy culinary lavender flowers from specialist lavender farms and online merchants. If you grow lavender yourself, you need to be sure the plants have never been sprayed with insecticide before you decide to cook with them.

6   Meanwhile, sterilize enough jars in the oven so that they are ready to use (see page 14).

7   Remove the pan from the heat and skim with a slotted spoon to remove any scum. Stir in the lavender extract. Leave to cool for 15 minutes (this will help to prevent the peel from rising in the jars).

8   Ladle the marmalade into the warmed, sterilized jars and cover immediately with a waxed disc and a dampened cellophane round or a lid. Label and store in a cool, dry, dark place. Refrigerate after opening.

Pink Grapefruit & Elderflower Marmalade

Grapefruit and elderflower complement each other very well, and make a refreshing marmalade. Pink grapefruit tends to be sweeter than yellow grapefruit, but you can use either in this recipe.

MAKES ABOUT: 2.7KG/6LB **PREPARATION TIME:** 45 MINUTES, PLUS 15 MINUTES COOLING
COOKING TIME: 1¾–2¼ HOURS

1kg/2lb 4oz pink grapefruits
500g/1lb 2oz lemons
1.3kg/3lb/scant 6 cups granulated sugar
6 tbsp elderflower cordial

1 Halve the grapefruits and lemons and squeeze out the juice and pips. Tie the pips, and any extra membrane that has come away during squeezing, in a piece of muslin/cheesecloth.

2 Either by hand or using the shredding attachment of a food processor, thinly slice the grapefruit and lemon peel, with its pith, into shreds.

3 Put the grapefruit and lemon juice and peel, the muslin bag and 1.75l/60fl oz/6⅔ cups water in a preserving pan and slowly bring to the boil. Reduce the heat and simmer gently for 1½–2 hours until the peel is soft and the liquid reduced by about half.

4 Remove the muslin bag from the pan and leave to cool for 5 minutes before squeezing it well and allowing the juices to run back into the pan. Discard the bag.

5 Add the sugar to the pan and stir until the sugar is completely dissolved. Bring to the boil and boil rapidly for about 15 minutes, or until setting point is reached. Test for a set either with a sugar thermometer (it should read 105°C/221°F) or put a teaspoon of the marmalade onto a cold saucer and leave to cool for a few minutes. If it wrinkles when you push it with your finger, then it is ready to use.

6 Meanwhile, sterilize enough jars in the oven so that they are ready to use (see page 14).

7 Remove the pan from the heat and skim with a slotted spoon to remove any scum. Stir in the elderflower cordial. Leave to cool for 15 minutes (this will help to prevent the peel from rising in the jars).

8 Ladle the marmalade into the warmed, sterilized jars and cover immediately with a waxed disc and a dampened cellophane round or a lid. Label and store in a cool, dry, dark place. Refrigerate after opening.

Orange & Cardamom Marmalade

With its floral notes, cardamom is a delicious addition to orange marmalade. Serve with warm croissants or brioche for breakfast.

MAKES ABOUT: 3KG/6LB 8OZ **PREPARATION TIME:** 50 MINUTES, PLUS 15 MINUTES COOLING
COOKING TIME: 1¾–2¼ HOURS

20 cardamom pods
1kg/2lb 4oz oranges
2 lemons
2kg/4lb 8oz/heaped 9 cups granulated sugar

1 Put the cardamom pods in a pestle and mortar and bash to crack the pods. Alternatively, use a wooden rolling pin. Tie in a piece of muslin/cheesecloth.

2 Halve the oranges and lemons and squeeze out the juice and pips. Tie the pips, and any extra membrane that has come away during squeezing, in another piece of muslin.

3 Either by hand or using the shredding attachment of a food processor, slice the orange and lemon peel, with its pith, into thin shreds.

4 Put the orange and lemon juice and peel, the muslin bags and 2.4l/84fl oz/9½ cups water in a preserving pan and slowly bring to the boil. Reduce the heat and simmer gently for 1½–2 hours until the peel is very soft and the liquid reduced by about half. Stir from time to time to prevent the mixture from sticking to the bottom of the pan.

5 Remove the muslin bags from the pan and leave to cool for 5 minutes before squeezing them well and allowing the juice to run back into the pan. Discard the bags.

6 Add the sugar to the pan and stir until completely dissolved. Bring to the boil and boil rapidly for about 15 minutes, or until setting point is reached. Test for a set either with a sugar thermometer (it should read 105°C/221°F) or put a teaspoon of the marmalade onto a cold saucer and leave to cool for a few minutes. If it wrinkles when you push it with your finger, then it is ready to use.

7 Meanwhile, sterilize enough jars in the oven so that they are ready to use (see page 14).

8 Remove the pan from the heat and skim with a slotted spoon to remove any scum. Leave to cool for 15 minutes (this will help to prevent the peel from rising in the jars).

9 Ladle the marmalade into the warmed, sterilized jars and cover immediately with a waxed disc and a dampened cellophane round or a lid. Label and store in a cool, dry, dark place. Refrigerate after opening.

Chunky Whisky Marmalade

A delicious combination that makes an excellent gift for whisky lovers. The recipe also works well with rum or brandy.

MAKES ABOUT: 3KG/6LB 8OZ **PREPARATION TIME:** 45 MINUTES, PLUS 15 MINUTES COOLING
COOKING TIME: 2¼ HOURS

1kg/2lb 4oz Seville oranges
juice of 2 lemons
2kg/4lb 8oz/heaped 9 cups granulated sugar
5 tbsp whisky

1 Halve the oranges and squeeze out the juice and pips. Tie the pips, and any extra membrane that has come away during squeezing, in a piece of muslin/cheesecloth.

2 By hand or using the shredding attachment of a food processor, slice the orange peel, with its pith, into thick, chunky shreds.

3 Put the orange juice and peel, the lemon juice, muslin bag and 2.4l/84fl oz/9½ cups water in a preserving pan and slowly bring to the boil. Reduce the heat and simmer gently for about 2 hours until the peel is really soft and the liquid reduced by about half.

4 Remove the muslin bag from the pan and leave to cool for 5 minutes before squeezing it well and allowing the juice to run back into the pan. Discard the bag.

5 Add the sugar to the pan and stir until completely dissolved. Bring to the boil and boil rapidly for about 15 minutes, or until setting point is reached. Test for a set either with a sugar thermometer (it should read 105°C/221°F) or put a teaspoon of the marmalade onto a cold saucer and leave to cool for a few minutes. If it wrinkles when you push it with your finger, then it is ready to use.

6 Meanwhile, sterilize enough jars in the oven so that they are ready to use (see page 14).

7 Remove the pan from the heat and skim with a slotted spoon to remove any scum. Stir in the whisky. Leave to cool for 15 minutes (this will help to prevent the peel from rising in the jars).

8 Ladle the marmalade into the warmed, sterilized jars and cover immediately with a waxed disc and a dampened cellophane round or a lid. Label and store in a cool, dry, dark place. Refrigerate after opening.

EMMA'S TIP If you like a dark, traditional marmalade, add 2 tablespoons treacle or replace 100g/3½oz/½ cup of the granulated sugar with soft dark brown sugar.

Jellies & Curds

Elderberry Jelly

To make this preserve you will need to gather wild elderberries in early to mid autumn when they are in season. Serve with roast meat dishes or try spooned on top of stewed apples. It is also lovely used to fill a Victoria sponge cake.

MAKES ABOUT: 6 X 225G/8OZ JARS **PREPARATION TIME:** 40 MINUTES, PLUS 24 HOURS STRAINING
COOKING TIME: 1 HOUR 20 MINUTES

1kg/2lb 4oz/8⅓ cups elderberries
1kg/2lb 4oz cooking apples
500g/1lb 2oz/2¼ cups granulated sugar per
   600ml/21fl oz/scant 2½ cups of extract

1　Remove any large stalks and the leaves from the elderberries. Without peeling or coring, roughly chop the apples into thick chunks, discarding any bruised or damaged pieces.

2　Put the elderberries and apples in a preserving pan and add 1.2l/40fl oz/4¾ cups water. Bring to the boil, then reduce the heat and simmer for 45–60 minutes until the fruits are soft and pulpy. Stir from time to time, to prevent the mixture from sticking to the bottom of the pan.

3　Meanwhile, prepare a scalded jelly bag or clean dish towel, attached to the legs of an upturned stool, with a large bowl underneath.

4　Pour the mixture into the bag and leave to drip into the bowl overnight or for at least 24 hours. Don't be tempted to push the pulp through the bag, or the jelly will be cloudy.

5　The next day, discard the pulp and measure the extract. Pour the extract into a preserving pan and for each 600ml/21fl oz/scant 2½ cups of extract, add 500g/1lb 2oz/2¼ cups sugar.

6　Meanwhile, sterilize enough jars in the oven so that they are ready to use (see page 14).

7　Gently heat the mixture, stirring all the time, until the sugar has dissolved. Bring to the boil and boil rapidly for about 10 minutes until setting point is reached. Test for a set either with a sugar thermometer (it should read 105°C/221°F) or put a teaspoon of the jelly onto a cold saucer and leave to cool for a few minutes. If it wrinkles when you push it with your finger, then it is ready to use.

8　Remove the pan from the heat and skim with a slotted spoon to remove any scum.

9　Ladle the jelly into the warmed, sterilized jars and cover immediately with a waxed disc and a dampened cellophane round or a lid. Label and store in a cool, dry, dark place. Refrigerate after opening.

Crab Apple Jelly

Crab apples are not available to buy commercially but you may have them growing in the garden or find them growing wild in parks and woodland. They make a pretty pink jelly that is particularly good served with roast pork or beef.

MAKES ABOUT: 6 X 225G/8OZ JARS **PREPARATION TIME:** 1¼ HOURS, PLUS 24 HOURS STRAINING
COOKING TIME: 1 HOUR 50 MINUTES

1.4kg/3lb 2oz crab apples
5 cloves or 2 star anise (optional)
500g/1lb 2oz/2¼ cups granulated sugar per
  600ml/21fl oz/scant 2½ cups of extract

1 Without peeling or coring, cut the crab apples into quarters, discarding any bruised or damaged pieces.

2 Put the chopped apples in a preserving pan and add enough water to cover them. If you like, add the cloves or star anise for added flavour. Bring to the boil, then reduce the heat and simmer gently for about 1½ hours until the crab apples are soft. Stir from time to time to prevent the mixture from sticking to the bottom of the pan.

3 Meanwhile, prepare a scalded jelly bag or clean dish towel, attached to the legs of an upturned stool, with a large bowl underneath.

4 Pour the mixture into the bag and leave to drip into the bowl overnight or for at least 24 hours. Don't be tempted to push the pulp through the bag, or the jelly will be cloudy.

5 The next day, discard the pulp and measure the extract. Pour the extract into a preserving pan and for each 600ml/21fl oz/scant 2½ cups of extract, add 500g/1lb 2oz/2¼ cups sugar.

6 Meanwhile, sterilize enough jars in the oven so that they are ready to use (see page 14).

7 Gently heat the mixture, stirring all the time, until the sugar has dissolved. Bring to the boil and boil rapidly for about 10 minutes until setting point is reached. Test for a set either with a sugar thermometer (it should read 105°C/221°F) or put a teaspoon of the jelly onto a cold saucer and leave to cool for a few minutes. If it wrinkles when you push it with your finger, then it is ready to use.

8 Remove the pan from the heat and skim with a slotted spoon to remove any scum.

9 Ladle the jelly into the warmed, sterilized jars and cover immediately with a waxed disc and a dampened cellophane round or a lid. Label and store in a cool, dry, dark place. Refrigerate after opening.

Mint Jelly

This is a fresh and tangy jelly to accompany roast lamb or sausages. You can also add it to salad dressings for a Moroccan twist. Make sage and rosemary jelly in the same way.

MAKES ABOUT: 6 X 225G/8OZ JARS **PREPARATION TIME:** 35 MINUTES PLUS 24 HOURS STRAINING
COOKING TIME: 1 HOUR 15 MINUTES

1.5kg/3lb 5oz cooking apples
2 large mint sprigs plus 6 tbsp chopped
    mint leaves
800ml/28fl oz/scant 3½ cups
    distilled white vinegar
500g/1lb 2oz/2¼ cups granulated sugar per
    600ml/21fl oz/scant 2½ cups of extract
green paste food colouring (optional)

1 Without peeling or coring, chop the apples into thick chunks, discarding any bruised or damaged pieces.

2 Put the chopped apples in a preserving pan and add 800ml/28fl oz/scant 3½ cups water and the mint sprigs. Bring to the boil, then reduce the heat and simmer for about 1 hour until the apples are soft and pulpy. Stir from time to time to prevent the mixture from sticking to the bottom of the pan.

3 Add the vinegar, return to the boil and boil for 5 minutes.

4 Meanwhile, prepare a scalded jelly bag or clean dish towel, attached to the legs of an upturned stool, with a large bowl underneath.

5 Pour the mixture into the bag and leave to drip into the bowl overnight or for at least 24 hours. Don't be tempted to push the pulp through the bag, or the jelly will be cloudy.

6 The next day, discard the pulp and measure the extract. Pour the extract into a preserving pan and for each 600ml/21fl oz/scant 2½ cups of extract, add 500g/1lb 2oz/2¼ cups sugar.

7 Meanwhile, sterilize enough jars in the oven so that they are ready to use (see page 14).

8 Gently heat the mixture, stirring all the time, until the sugar has dissolved. Bring to the boil and boil rapidly for about 10 minutes until setting point is reached. Test for a set either with a sugar thermometer (it should read 105°C/221°F) or put a teaspoon of the jelly onto a cold saucer and leave to cool for a few minutes. If it wrinkles when you push it with your finger, then it is ready to use.

9 Remove the pan from the heat and skim with a slotted spoon to remove any scum. Stir in the chopped mint and colour the mixture a shade of green by adding a tiny drop of food colouring, if using.

10 Ladle the jelly into the warmed, sterilized jars and cover immediately with a waxed disc and a dampened cellophane round or a lid. Label and store in a cool, dry, dark place. Refrigerate after opening.

Hot Chilli Jelly

This is for those who like something hot and fiery with cold meats, sausages or burgers. One of the staff at Bay Tree recommends this jelly eaten with natural yogurt.

MAKES ABOUT: 4 X 225G/8OZ JARS **PREPARATION TIME:** 45 MINUTES, PLUS 24 HOURS STRAINING AND 10 MINUTES COOLING **COOKING TIME:** 1 HOUR 10 MINUTES

1kg/2lb 4oz cooking apples
9–10 red chillies, finely chopped
500ml/17fl oz/2 cups red wine vinegar
500g/1lb 2oz/2¼ cups granulated sugar per
   600ml/21fl oz/scant 2½ cups of extract

1 Without peeling or coring, roughly chop the apples into thick, medium chunks, discarding any bruised or damaged pieces.

2 Put the chopped apples in a preserving pan and add 500ml/17fl oz/2 cups water and 6 of the chopped chillies, with their seeds. Bring to the boil, then reduce the heat and simmer for about 45 minutes until the apples are soft and pulpy. Stir from time to time to prevent the mixture from sticking to the bottom of the pan.

3 Add the vinegar, return to the boil and boil for 5 minutes.

4 Meanwhile, prepare a scalded jelly bag or clean dish towel, attached to the legs of an upturned stool, with a large bowl underneath.

5 Pour the mixture into the bag and leave to drip into the bowl overnight or for at least 24 hours. Don't be tempted to push the pulp through the bag, or the jelly will be cloudy.

6 The next day, discard the pulp and measure the extract. Pour the extract into a preserving pan and for each 600ml/21fl oz/scant 2½ cups of extract, add 500g/1lb 2oz/2¼ cups sugar.

7 Meanwhile, sterilize enough jars in the oven so that they are ready to use (see page 14).

8 Gently heat the mixture, stirring all the time, until the sugar has dissolved. Bring to the boil and boil rapidly for about 10 minutes until setting point is reached. Test for a set either with a sugar thermometer (it should read 105°C/221°F) or put a teaspoon of the jelly onto a cold saucer and leave to cool for a few minutes. If it wrinkles when you push it with your finger, then it is ready to use.

9 Remove the pan from the heat and skim with a slotted spoon to remove any scum. Stir in the remaining chillies, without the seeds. Leave the jelly to cool for 10 minutes (this will help to prevent the chilli from rising in the jars).

10 Ladle the jelly into the warmed, sterilized jars and cover immediately with a waxed disc and a dampened cellophane round or a lid. Label and store in a cool, dry, dark place. Refrigerate after opening.

Black Pepper & Cumin Jelly

Serve this jelly with soft cheese or cold meats, or alternatively use as an ingredient in casseroles, gravies and stir-fries, or as a glaze on grilled meats.

MAKES ABOUT: 4 X 225G/8OZ JARS **PREPARATION TIME:** 50 MINUTES, PLUS 24 HOURS STRAINING AND 10 MINUTES COOLING **COOKING TIME:** 1 HOUR 10 MINUTES

1kg/2lb 4oz cooking apples
2 tbsp black peppercorns, lightly crushed
2 tbsp cumin seeds, lightly crushed
500ml/17fl oz/2 cups apple cider vinegar
500g/1lb 2oz/2¼ cups granulated sugar per 600ml/21fl oz/scant 2½ cups of extract

1 Without peeling or coring, roughly chop the apples into thick, medium chunks, discarding any bruised or damaged pieces.

2 Put the chopped apples in a preserving pan and add 500ml/17fl oz/2 cups water, 1 tablespoon of the peppercorns and 1 tablespoon of the cumin seeds. Bring to the boil, then reduce the heat and simmer for about 45 minutes until the apples are soft and pulpy. Stir from time to time to prevent the mixture from sticking to the bottom of the pan.

3 Add the vinegar, return to the boil and boil for 5 minutes.

4 Meanwhile, prepare a scalded jelly bag or clean dish towel, attached to the legs of an upturned stool, with a large bowl underneath.

5 Pour the mixture into the bag and leave to drip into the bowl overnight or for at least 24 hours. Don't be tempted to push the pulp through the bag, or the jelly will be cloudy.

6 The next day, discard the pulp and measure the extract. Pour the extract into a preserving pan and for each 600ml/21fl oz/scant 2½ cups of extract, add 500g/1lb 2oz/2¼ cups sugar.

7 Meanwhile, sterilize enough jars in the oven so that they are ready to use (see page 14).

8 Gently heat the mixture, stirring all the time, until the sugar has dissolved. Bring to the boil and boil rapidly for about 10 minutes until setting point is reached. Test for a set either with a sugar thermometer (it should read 105°C/221°F) or put a teaspoon of the jelly onto a cold saucer and leave to cool for a few minutes. If it wrinkles when you push it with your finger, then it is ready to use.

9 Remove the pan from the heat and skim with a slotted spoon to remove any scum. Stir in the remaining peppercorns and cumin seeds. Leave the jelly to cool for 10 minutes (this will help to prevent the spices from rising in the jars).

10 Ladle the jelly into the warmed, sterilized jars and cover immediately with a waxed disc and a dampened cellophane round or a lid. Label and store in a cool, dry, dark place. Refrigerate after opening.

Passion Fruit Curd

Intensely scented, this is passion fruit captured in a jar. For a delicious, super-quick dessert, serve a large dollop of this curd on top of Greek yogurt and add a generous sprinkling of blueberries.

MAKES ABOUT: 600G/1LB 5OZ **PREPARATION TIME:** 30 MINUTES **COOKING TIME:** 25 MINUTES

6 passion fruits
50g/1¾oz unsalted butter,
   cut into small pieces
120g/4¼oz/heaped ½ cup granulated sugar
2 large eggs

1 Cut the passion fruits in half and scoop out the flesh into a sieve standing over a bowl. Using a wooden spoon, push the flesh into the bowl. Reserve 1 tablespoon of the seeds and discard the rest.

2 Sterilize enough small jars in the oven so that they are ready to use (see page 14).

3 Put the passion fruit juice, butter and sugar in a double boiler or a heatproof bowl. Rest the bowl, if using, over a saucepan of gently simmering water. Stir the mixture until the sugar has dissolved and the butter has melted.

4 Break the eggs into a bowl and, using a balloon whisk, beat together well. Whisk the eggs into the butter mixture.

5 Heat gently and cook for about 20 minutes, whisking frequently, until the mixture is thick enough to coat the back of a wooden spoon. Do not allow the mixture to boil or it will curdle. If the curd does start to split, remove from the heat and whisk vigorously until smooth.

6 Stir in the reserved passion fruit seeds to add crunch and colour to the curd.

7 Pour the curd into the warmed, sterilized jars. Cover immediately with a waxed disc and a dampened cellophane round or a lid, and label. Leave to cool completely before storing in the refrigerator for up to 2 weeks. Once opened, eat within 3 days.

EMMA'S TIP Like all curds, you have to be patient when making this recipe. Don't be tempted to turn the heat up too high as the mixture might curdle. You will need to whisk until the mixture is thick; this can take from 20–40 minutes.

Very Lemon Curd

The title describes this curd perfectly. Packed with lemon zest, it is ideal for spreading thickly on toast or crumpets or as a filling for a cake or a lemon tart. And who can resist devouring it straight from the jar?

MAKES ABOUT: 800G/1LB 12OZ **PREPARATION TIME:** 30 MINUTES **COOKING TIME:** 25 MINUTES

grated zest and juice of 4 lemons
175g/6oz unsalted butter,
   cut into small pieces
270g/9½oz/1¼ cups granulated sugar
4 large eggs

1 Sterilize enough small jars in the oven so that they are ready to use (see page 14).

2 Strain the lemon juice into a double boiler or a heatproof bowl. Rest the bowl, if using, over a saucepan of gently simmering water so that the bottom of the bowl does not touch the water.

3 Add the lemon zest, butter and sugar and heat gently, stirring the mixture until the sugar has dissolved and the butter has melted.

4 Break the eggs into a bowl and, using a balloon whisk, beat together well. Whisk the eggs into the butter mixture.

5 Heat gently and cook for about 20 minutes, whisking frequently, until the mixture is thick enough to coat the back of a wooden spoon. Do not allow the mixture to boil or it will curdle. If the curd does start to split, remove from the heat and whisk vigorously until smooth.

6 Pour the curd into the warmed, sterilized jars. Cover immediately with a waxed disc and a dampened cellophane round or a lid, and label. Leave to cool completely before storing in the refrigerator for up to 2 weeks. Once opened, eat within 3 days.

EMMA'S TIP To make Lime Curd, replace the lemons with the zest and juice from 6 limes. You could also try a mixture of lemons and limes together.

Raspberry Curd

Serve this luxurious, buttery curd spread on toast or use it to sandwich a chocolate or vanilla sponge cake together. You can use blackberries instead of raspberries and cook in the same way. Both will also be delicious used to fill a tart as a change from lemon curd.

MAKES ABOUT: 680G/1LB 8OZ **PREPARATION TIME:** 40 MINUTES **COOKING TIME:** 30 MINUTES

600g/1lb 5oz/4¾ cups raspberries
1 tbsp orange juice
150g/5½oz unsalted butter,
    cut into small pieces
250g/9oz/scant 1¼ cups granulated sugar
4 large eggs

1 Sterilize enough small jars in the oven so that they are ready to use (see page 14).

2 Put the raspberries and orange juice in a saucepan. Heat the mixture gently and simmer for 5 minutes until the juices start to run and the fruit is very soft.

3 Using the back of a wooden spoon, push the cooked raspberries through a sieve into a double boiler or a heatproof bowl. Rest the bowl, if using, over a saucepan of gently simmering water so that the bottom of the bowl does not touch the water.

4 Add the butter and sugar to the pan and heat gently, stirring the mixture until the sugar has dissolved and the butter has melted.

5 Break the eggs into a bowl and, using a balloon whisk, beat together well. Whisk the eggs into the butter mixture.

6 Heat gently and cook for about 20 minutes, whisking frequently, until the mixture is thick enough to coat the back of a wooden spoon. Do not allow the mixture to boil or it will curdle. If the curd does start to split, remove from the heat and whisk vigorously until smooth.

7 Pour the curd into the warmed, sterilized jars. Cover immediately with a waxed disc and a dampened cellophane round or a lid, and label. Leave to cool completely before storing in the refrigerator for up to 2 weeks. Once opened, eat within 3 days.

Tangerine Curd

A twist on traditional lemon curd, this curd is still rich but has a sweeter flavour. It is delicious used to fill pastries or spread on toast, scones or muffins. An alternative to tangerines are clementines (sometimes called seedless tangerines) or satsumas, which are types of mandarins varying in their sweetness. Oranges, too, can be used. Whichever fruit you choose, don't expect the curd to be bright orange, as the colour of the curd comes from the egg yolks rather than the fruit juice.

MAKES ABOUT: 625G/1LB 6OZ **PREPARATION TIME:** 30 MINUTES **COOKING TIME:** 25 MINUTES

grated zest and juice of 4 tangerines
125g/4½oz unsalted butter,
   cut into small pieces
200g/7oz/scant 1 cup granulated sugar
3 large eggs

1 Sterilize enough small jars in the oven so that they are ready to use (see page 14).

2 Strain the tangerine juice into a double boiler or a heatproof bowl. Rest the bowl, if using, over a saucepan of gently simmering water.

3 Add the tangerine zest, butter and sugar to the pan and heat gently, stirring the mixture until the sugar has dissolved and the butter has melted.

4 Break the eggs into a bowl and, using a balloon whisk, beat together well. Whisk the eggs into the butter mixture.

5 Heat gently and cook for about 20 minutes, whisking frequently, until the mixture is thick enough to coat the back of a wooden spoon. Do not allow the mixture to boil or it will curdle. If the curd does start to split, remove from the heat and whisk vigorously until smooth.

6 Pour the curd into the warmed, sterilized jars. Cover immediately with a waxed disc and a dampened cellophane round or a lid, and label. Leave to cool completely before storing in the refrigerator for up to 2 weeks. Once opened, eat within 3 days.

EMMA'S TIP If you prefer a very tangy flavour to your curd, replace 1 tangerine with the grated zest and juice of 1 lemon, which cuts through the sweetness of the tangerine.

Coconut Curd

A popular preserve in Malaysia, Singapore and Indonesia is kaya, also known as coconut curd or coconut egg jam. Similar to a curd, the authentic product uses fresh pandan leaves, which have a pine and citrus taste. As these can usually only be found in Asian supermarkets, the recipe includes them as optional – it is delicious with or without them. The curd is served as a snack spread on buttered toast.

MAKES ABOUT: 300G/10½OZ **PREPARATION TIME:** 20 MINUTES **COOKING TIME:** 25 MINUTES

200ml/7fl oz/scant 1 cup coconut milk
50g/1¾oz/¼ cup palm sugar
50g/1¾oz/¼ cup granulated sugar
4 fresh pandan/screwpine leaves (optional)
4 large eggs

1 Sterilize enough small jars in the oven so that they are ready to use (see page 14).

2 Put the coconut milk, palm and granulated sugars, and pandan leaves, if using, in a double boiler or a heatproof bowl. Rest the bowl, if using, over a saucepan of gently simmering water. Stir the mixture until all the sugar has dissolved.

3 Break the eggs into a bowl and, using a balloon whisk, beat together well. Whisk the eggs into the coconut mixture.

4 Heat gently and cook for about 20 minutes, whisking frequently, until the mixture is thick enough to coat the back of a wooden spoon. Do not allow the mixture to boil or it will curdle. If the curd does start to split, remove from the heat and whisk vigorously until smooth.

5 Remove the pandan leaves, if used.

6 Pour the curd into the warmed, sterilized jars. Cover immediately with a waxed disc and a dampened cellophane round or a lid, and label. Leave to cool completely before storing in the refrigerator for up to 2 weeks. Once opened, eat within 3 days.

Very Ginger Curd

Packed with fresh and stem ginger, just the smell of this luxurious curd will make you reach for a spoon! It is perfect on toast or crumpets, or use it to sandwich together ginger biscuits or cookies.

MAKES ABOUT: 680G/1LB 8OZ **PREPARATION TIME:** 30 MINUTES **COOKING TIME:** 25 MINUTES

juice of 2 lemons
50g/1¾oz fresh ginger, peeled and grated
3 tbsp medium-dry white wine
100g/3½oz unsalted butter,
   cut into small pieces
300g/10½oz/1⅓ cups granulated sugar
4 large eggs
60g/2¼oz stem/preserved ginger,
   finely chopped

1 Sterilize enough small jars in the oven so that they are ready to use (see page 14).
2 Strain the lemon juice into a double boiler or a heatproof bowl. Rest the bowl, if using, over a saucepan of gently simmering water.
3 Add the freshly grated ginger, wine, butter and sugar to the pan and heat gently, stirring the mixture until the sugar has dissolved and the butter has melted.
4 Break the eggs into a bowl and, using a balloon whisk, beat together well. Whisk the eggs into the butter mixture.
5 Heat gently and cook for about 20 minutes, whisking frequently, until the mixture is thick enough to coat the back of a wooden spoon. Do not allow the mixture to boil or it will curdle. If the curd does start to split, remove from the heat and whisk vigorously until smooth.
6 Stir the stem ginger into the mixture.
7 Pour the curd into the warmed, sterilized jars. Cover immediately with a waxed disc and a dampened cellophane round or a lid, and label. Leave to cool completely before storing in the refrigerator for up to 2 weeks. Once opened, eat within 3 days.

EMMA'S TIP Store fresh ginger in the freezer rather than the refrigerator so that you always have a fresh piece when needed. When you come to use it, simply grate as much as you need. It is not even necessary to thaw it first.

Le Nièr Beurre

Black butter, a traditional delicacy from Jersey (the largest of the Channel Islands), was usually made in autumn, when groups of men and children would gather the apples while the women peeled them. It is rich, spicy and dark, as its name suggests. Serve spread on fresh crusty bread or as an accompaniment to cold meats.

MAKES ABOUT: 1.9KG/4LB 3OZ **PREPARATION TIME:** 30 MINUTES **COOKING TIME:** 2 HOURS

1l/34fl oz/4 cups cider/hard cider
1.3kg/3lb eating apples, peeled,
    cored and sliced
grated zest and juice of 1 lemon
4cm/1½in piece of liquorice stick,
    very finely chopped
350g/12oz/scant 1⅔ cups granulated sugar
    per 600ml/21fl oz/scant 2½ cups of purée
2 tsp ground cinnamon
1 tsp ground allspice
½ tsp ground cloves

1 Pour the cider into a large, heavy-based saucepan, bring to the boil and boil rapidly for about 20 minutes until reduced by half.

2 Add the apple slices and simmer for about 40 minutes until the apples are soft and pulpy. Stir from time to time to prevent the mixture from sticking to the bottom of the pan.

3 Add the lemon zest and juice and liquorice and continue to cook for 5 minutes until the mixture is well reduced and there is no excess liquid in the pan.

4 Measure the purée and return to the cleaned pan. For each 600ml/21fl oz/scant 2½ cups of purée add 350g/12oz/scant 1⅔ cups sugar. Add the cinnamon, allspice and cloves.

5 Heat gently, stirring all the time, until the sugar has dissolved. Continue cooking for about 1 hour until the mixture is a thick spreading consistency. Stir frequently and keep the heat low, as the mixture tends to spit.

6 Meanwhile, sterilize enough small jars in the oven so that they are ready to use (see page 14).

7 Pour the butter into the warmed, sterilized jars and cover immediately with a waxed disc and a dampened cellophane round or a lid. Label and store in a cool, dry, dark place for at least 3 months before eating, to allow the butter to mature and darken. Refrigerate after opening.

Apricot & Orange Butter

Fresh apricots combine beautifully with oranges. Serve this butter spread thickly on croissants, buttery brioche, coarse wholemeal toast or pancakes for a delicious breakfast. You will be tempted to eat several of whatever you choose!

MAKES ABOUT: 1KG/2LB 4OZ **PREPARATION TIME:** 30 MINUTES **COOKING TIME:** 1 HOUR 35 MINUTES

1kg/2lb 4oz apricots, pitted
grated zest and juice of 2 oranges
350g/12oz/scant 1⅔ cups granulated sugar
**   per 600ml/21fl oz/scant 2½ cups of purée**

1 Put the apricots, orange zest and juice in a large saucepan and add 300ml/10½fl oz/scant 1¼ cups water. Bring to the boil, then reduce the heat and simmer gently for about 45 minutes until the apricots are soft and pulpy.

2 Using a wooden spoon, push the mixture through a sieve into a large jug/pitcher or a bowl.

3 Measure the purée and return to the cleaned pan. For each 600ml/21fl oz/scant 2½ cups of purée add 350g/12oz/scant 1⅔ cups sugar.

4 Heat gently, stirring all the time, until the sugar has dissolved. Bring to the boil and boil rapidly for 30–40 minutes until the mixture is a thick spreading consistency. Stir frequently to prevent the mixture from sticking to the bottom of the pan.

5 Meanwhile, sterilize enough small jars in the oven so that they are ready to use (see page 14).

6 Pour the butter into the warmed, sterilized jars and cover immediately with a waxed disc and a dampened cellophane round or a lid. Label and store in a cool, dry, dark place. Refrigerate after opening.

EMMA'S TIP Fruit butters and cheeses are easy to make but puréeing the fruit can be hard work. To help speed matters up, crush the fruit with a potato masher or fork when soft and then push it through the sieve in small batches.

Damson Cheese

A lovely way to use a glut of damsons, this cheese can also be made with any small plums you have. You can make apple cheese in the same way by replacing the damsons with apples and the allspice with ½ teaspoon ground cinnamon and ¼ teaspoon ground cloves. Alternatively, use a mixture of half apples and half blackberries for a stunning, dark bramble cheese. All can be served with cheese, pâtés, cold meats or roast pork.

MAKES ABOUT: 1KG/2LB 4OZ **PREPARATION TIME:** 25 MINUTES **COOKING TIME:** 1 HOUR 10 MINUTES

1kg/2lb 4oz damsons
500g/1lb 2oz/2¼ cups granulated sugar per
600ml/21fl oz/scant 2½ cups of purée
½ tsp ground allspice
mild-flavoured olive oil or glycerine,
for brushing

1 Put the damsons in a large, heavy-based saucepan and add enough water to just cover the fruit. Bring to the boil, then reduce the heat and simmer gently for about 20 minutes until the plums are soft. Scoop out the stones/pits with a slotted spoon as they rise to the surface.

2 Using a wooden spoon, push the mixture through a sieve into a large jug/pitcher or a bowl.

3 Measure the purée and return to the cleaned pan. For each 600ml/21fl oz/scant 2½ cups of purée add 500g/1lb 2oz/2¼ cups sugar. Add the allspice.

4 Heat gently, stirring all the time, until the sugar has dissolved. Bring to the boil and boil rapidly for 30–40 minutes until the mixture is a thick spreading consistency. Stir frequently to prevent the mixture from sticking to the bottom of the pan. The cheese is ready when a wooden spoon drawn across the base of the pan reveals it cleanly.

5 Meanwhile, brush the insides of a small bowl or small, straight-sided individual moulds or ramekin dishes with a little olive oil.

6 Spoon the cheese into the prepared dishes and level the surface. Cover the surface with a waxed disc and a dampened cellophane round.

7 Store the cheese in the refrigerator for at least 1 month before eating, to allow the cheese to mature.

8 To serve, turn the cheese out of its dish and serve whole, sliced into small portions. Eat within 1 year.

EMMA'S TIP Like all fruit cheeses, this is extremely good served with a cheeseboard, but an alternative way of serving it is to cut it into cubes, lightly sprinkle with granulated sugar and eat just as it is.

Membrillo

This traditional quince cheese is known as membrillo in Spain, marmelado in Portugal and pâté de coings in France. In the 13th century, fruit cheeses were known as 'marmalades', which is from the Portuguese word for quince. Serve membrillo with a single cheese such as Manchego (a hard Spanish cheese) or a cheeseboard.

MAKES ABOUT: 1KG/2LB 4OZ **PREPARATION TIME:** 35 MINUTES **COOKING TIME:** 1 HOUR 20 MINUTES

1kg/2lb 4oz quinces
500g/1lb 2oz/2¼ cups granulated sugar per
   600ml/21fl oz/scant 2½ cups of purée
mild-flavoured olive oil or glycerine,
   for brushing

1 Without peeling or coring, chop the quinces, discarding any bruised or damaged pieces.

2 Put the chopped quinces in a large, heavy-based saucepan and add 300ml/10½fl oz/scant 1¼ cups water to just cover the fruit. Bring to the boil, then reduce the heat and simmer gently for about 30 minutes until the quinces are soft and pulpy. Stir from time to time to prevent the mixture from sticking to the bottom of the pan.

3 Using a wooden spoon, push the mixture through a sieve into a large jug/pitcher or a bowl.

4 Measure the purée and return to the cleaned pan. For each 600ml/21fl oz/scant 2½ cups of purée add 500g/1lb 2oz/2¼ cups sugar.

5 Heat gently, stirring all the time, until the sugar has dissolved. Bring to the boil and boil rapidly for 30–40 minutes until the mixture is a thick spreading consistency. Stir frequently to prevent the mixture from sticking to the bottom of the pan. The cheese is ready when a wooden spoon drawn across the base of the pan reveals it cleanly.

6 Meanwhile, brush the insides of a small bowl or small, straight-sided individual moulds or ramekin dishes with a little olive oil.

7 Spoon the cheese into the prepared dishes and level the surface. Cover the surface with a waxed disc and a dampened cellophane round.

8 Store the cheese in the refrigerator for at least 1 month before eating, to allow the cheese to mature.

9 To serve, turn the cheese out of its dish and serve whole, sliced into small portions. Eat within 1 year.

Conserved & Bottled

Snapdragon

You may wonder how this conserve came to have its name but I don't know! It is probably because of the game Snapdragon (see below). We like to eat it straight from the jar with a long fork at Christmas time or as a winter fruit salad.

MAKES ABOUT: 1.5KG/3LB 5OZ **PREPARATION TIME:** 20 MINUTES **COOKING TIME:** 10 MINUTES

200ml/7fl oz/scant 1 cup rum
250g/9oz/heaped 1⅓ cups dried apricots
250g/9oz/heaped 1½ cups dried figs
250g/9oz/2 cups raisins
250g/9oz/scant 1¼ cups granulated sugar
grated zest and juice of 1 lemon
grated zest and juice of 1 orange
60g/2¼oz/heaped ⅓ cup blanched almonds

1 Sterilize enough jars in the oven so that they are ready to use (see page 14).

2 Put the rum and 200ml/7fl oz/scant 1 cup water in a large, heavy-based saucepan. Add all the remaining ingredients, except the almonds.

3 Cover the pan and slowly bring to the boil. Stir the ingredients together well, reduce the heat and simmer for 5 minutes.

4 Remove the pan from the heat and half-fill the warmed, sterilized jars with the conserve. Using about 15 almonds for each jar, arrange the almonds in a layer on top of the conserve and then top with the remaining conserve to fill the jars.

5 Cover immediately with a waxed disc and a dampened cellophane round or a lid. Label and store in a cool, dry, dark place. Refrigerate after opening.

EMMA'S TIP If you wish to find your true love, you could play the game Snapdragon. Also known as Flapdragon, this Victorian parlour game involved raisins being snatched from a bowl of burning brandy and eaten, at the risk of burning mouths. The traditional belief was that the person who snatched the most fruits would meet their true love within the year. The game was played in England, the United States and Canada during the winter months, particularly at Christmas and Halloween.

Strawberry Conserve

This soft-set, whole strawberry conserve is best served spooned, rather than spread. It is delicious served on top of meringues, or on warm scones with a large spoonful of thick clotted cream or crème fraîche.

MAKES ABOUT: 1KG/2LB 4OZ **PREPARATION TIME:** 15 MINUTES, PLUS 48 HOURS MACERATING AND 15 MINUTES COOLING **COOKING TIME:** 20 MINUTES

1kg/2lb 4oz small strawberries
1kg/2lb 4oz/4½ cups granulated sugar
juice of 2 lemons

1 In a large bowl, put the strawberries and sugar in layers. Cover and leave to macerate at room temperature for 24 hours.

2 The next day, put the mixture in a saucepan, slowly bring to the boil, stirring until the sugar dissolves, then boil for 5 minutes until the strawberries have softened but not broken up.

3 Return the mixture to the bowl, cover and leave at room temperature for a further 24 hours.

4 Sterilize enough jars in the oven so that they are ready to use (see page 14).

5 Return the mixture to the pan and add the lemon juice. Bring to the boil and then boil for 5–10 minutes until setting point is reached. Test for a set either with a sugar thermometer (it should read 105°C/221°F) or put a teaspoon of the conserve onto a cold saucer and leave until completely cool for a few minutes. If it wrinkles when you push it with your finger, then it is ready to use.

6 Remove the pan from the heat and leave to cool for 15 minutes (this will help to prevent the strawberries from rising in the jars).

7 Ladle the conserve into the warmed, sterilized jars. Cover immediately with a waxed disc and a dampened cellophane round or a lid. Label and store in a cool, dry, dark place. Eat within 3 months and refrigerate after opening.

EMMA'S TIP Leaving the strawberries in sugar helps to draw out their juices and keep them whole during cooking. It is important to use small, juicy whole strawberries, when they are in season.

Bar-le-Duc

This redcurrant conserve originated from Bar-le-Duc in the Lorraine region of France. In the authentic recipe, the seeds of the currants are removed, but it is just as delicious if this time-consuming task is not done. Serve it on thin toast or, as they do in France, with madeleine cakes or as the dessert known as Duchesse-le-Duc. This is scoops of vanilla ice cream, surrounded by a skirt of Bar-le-Duc, served with sweetened whipped cream and decorated with sugared violets.

MAKES ABOUT: 1.25KG/2LB 12OZ **PREPARATION TIME:** 20 MINUTES, PLUS 24 HOURS MACERATING AND 30 MINUTES COOLING **COOKING TIME:** 5 MINUTES

500g/1lb 2oz/heaped 4 cups redcurrants,
  stripped
750g/1lb 10oz/heaped 3⅓ cups
  granulated sugar

1 Put the redcurrants in a bowl, add the sugar and stir together. Cover and leave to macerate at room temperature for 24 hours.

2 The next day, put the mixture in a saucepan, slowly bring to the boil and boil for 3 minutes. Remove the pan from the heat and leave to cool for 30 minutes until a skin starts to form.

3 Meanwhile, sterilize enough jars in the oven so that they are ready to use (see page 14).

4 Gently stir the mixture to evenly distribute the redcurrants and then ladle the conserve into the warmed, sterilized jars. Cover immediately with a waxed disc and a dampened cellophane round or a lid. Label and store in a cool, dry, dark place. Eat within 3 months and refrigerate after opening.

EMMA'S TIP It is not essential to deseed redcurrants, but if you have time, prick each redcurrant with a sewing needle to help them remain plump during cooking.

Raspberry & Kirsch Conserve

Whole raspberries, suspended in a kirsch syrup, are the perfect preserve to have tucked away to serve at a moment's notice. Add a spoonful to vanilla ice cream, Greek yogurt or fromage frais for an instant dessert.

MAKES ABOUT: 1KG/2LB 4OZ **PREPARATION TIME:** 20 MINUTES, PLUS 1 HOUR 20 MINUTES STANDING
COOKING TIME: 15 MINUTES

1kg/2lb 4oz/8 cups raspberries
1kg/2lb 4oz/4½ cups granulated sugar
2 tbsp kirsch

1 Preheat the oven to 180°C/350°F/Gas 4.
2 Put the raspberries on a baking sheet in a single layer. Sprinkle the sugar on a separate baking sheet and bake both sheets for 15 minutes.
3 Turn the raspberries and sugar into a large bowl and gently stir together until combined. Leave to stand for 20 minutes. Repeat the stirring and standing three more times.
4 Meanwhile, sterilize enough jars in the oven so that they are ready to use (see page 14).
5 Stir the kirsch into the raspberry mixture.
6 Ladle the conserve into the warmed, sterilized jars. Cover immediately with a waxed disc and a dampened cellophane round or a lid. Label and store in a cool, dry, dark place. Eat within 3 months and refrigerate after opening.

EMMA'S TIP Kirsch, an abbreviation of its full name Kirschwasser, originated in Germany. It is a clear, colourless fruit brandy made from cherries. It is not sweet (unlike cherry brandies) and has a subtle, sour cherry and almond flavour, which comes from the cherry stones/pits. Kirsch complements raspberries beautifully, but other liqueurs such as framboise (made from raspberries), brandy and cherry brandy can be used instead for this recipe.

Apricot & Orange Mincemeat

This luscious mincemeat is packed with plump apricots and orange, with a subtle hint of sherry, too. It makes a delicious change from the usual mincemeat that you buy. Use it to fill pies or baked apples.

MAKES ABOUT: 2KG/4LB 8OZ **PREPARATION TIME:** 25 MINUTES, PLUS 48 HOURS MACERATING AND 2 WEEKS MATURING

250g/9oz/heaped 1⅓ cups dried apricots
grated zest and juice of 2 large oranges
750g/1lb 10oz/4⅓ cups mixed dried fruit
100g/3½oz/½ cup candied orange peel
200ml/7fl oz/scant 1 cup sherry
4 tbsp orange marmalade
500g/1lb 2oz/2¼ cups Demerara sugar
250g/9oz/2 cups shredded beef or
   vegetable suet
1 tbsp ground mixed spice/pumpkin pie spice

1 Using scissors, cut the apricots into small pieces and put in a large bowl. Add the grated orange zest and juice. Put the dried fruit and candied orange peel in a separate large bowl and add the sherry. Cover both bowls and leave to macerate for 24 hours.

2 The next day, combine the soaked apricots and dried fruits together. Add the orange marmalade, sugar, suet and mixed spice and stir well together. Cover the bowl and leave for a further 24 hours.

3 Sterilize enough jars in the oven so that they are ready to use (see page 14).

4 Pack the mincemeat into the warmed, sterilized jars, taking care not to leave any air bubbles. Cover immediately with a waxed disc and a dampened cellophane round or a lid. Label and store in a cool, dry, dark place.

5 Leave to mature for at least 2 weeks before using. Refrigerate after opening.

EMMA'S TIP Dried apricots come in various shapes and forms. For this recipe, choose natural dried apricots that haven't been pre-soaked. Dark, dried apricots (dark because they haven't been treated with sulphur dioxide) may not look as attractive but their flavour is much more intense than bland, plumper apricots.

Boozy Cherry & Walnut Mincemeat

Vine fruits that are soaked in sherry for several days make this a heady mixture, and all the more delicious with juicy cherries and crunchy walnuts. Perfect for baked apples and pies. The longer you leave it to mature, the better.

MAKES ABOUT: 1.8KG/4LB **PREPARATION TIME:** 15 MINUTES, PLUS 48 HOURS MACERATING AND 2 WEEKS MATURING

250g/9oz firm cooking apples, peeled, cored and grated
275g/9¾oz/1⅓ cups glacé/candied cherries, halved
100g/3½oz/1 cup walnuts, roughly chopped
500g/1lb 2oz/3 cups mixed dried vine fruit
375g/13oz/scant 1¾ cups Demerara sugar
100g/3½oz/¾ cup shredded beef or vegetable suet
1 tsp ground mixed spice/pumpkin pie spice
300ml/10½fl oz/scant 1¼ cups sherry

1 Put all the ingredients in a large bowl and stir well together. Cover the bowl and leave to macerate for 48 hours. Stir the mixture occasionally as you pass.

2 Sterilize enough jars in the oven so that they are ready to use (see page 14).

3 Pack the mincemeat into the warmed, sterilized jars, taking care not to leave any air bubbles. Cover immediately with a waxed disc and a dampened cellophane round or a lid. Label and store in a cool, dry, dark place.

4 Leave to mature for at least 2 weeks before using. Refrigerate after opening.

EMMA'S TIP Mincemeat was originally a method of preserving meat in alcohol. By the middle of the 20th century, meat was no longer preserved in this way, and the mincemeat we know today developed. Beef suet is an ingredient of the past and can appear in traditional recipes. Solid vegetable suet is often used instead now, making it suitable for vegetarians. You can choose to use either in this recipe.

Golden Clementines

Glistening whole clementines not only look stunning packed in a jar but they are wonderful to eat, too. They would be a lovely gift, in which case pack them into two smaller jars so that you have one to keep. Serve them as a dessert spooned on top of ice cream, Greek yogurt, crème fraîche or ricotta cheese.

MAKES ABOUT: 1L/34FL OZ **PREPARATION TIME:** 40 MINUTES, PLUS 1 HOUR SOAKING AND 2–3 HOURS COOLING, PLUS BOTTLING (OPTIONAL) **COOKING TIME:** 25 MINUTES

10 clementines
200g/7oz/scant 1 cup granulated sugar

1 Remove the zest from the clementines, cut into thick strips and put in a small saucepan. Add 170ml/5½fl oz/⅔ cup water and leave to soak for 1 hour.

2 Sterilize a 1l/34fl oz preserving jar so that it is ready to use (see page 14).

3 Peel the clementines and, using the tip of a sharp knife, remove all the white pith. Take care when doing this so that the clementines will look attractive when preserved.

4 Pack the clementines into the warmed, sterilized jar, arranging them attractively.

5 When the clementine zest has soaked, heat gently and simmer for 10 minutes.

6 Strain the liquid into a clean, heavy-based saucepan and add the sugar. Heat gently, stirring until the sugar has dissolved. Bring to the boil and boil rapidly for 5–10 minutes until the liquid turns a pale golden colour.

7 Pour the syrup into a heatproof measuring jug/cup and make up to 450ml/16fl oz/2 cups with water. Leave for 2–3 hours until completely cold.

8 Pour the cold syrup over the clementines, covering them completely. Leave a 1cm/½in gap between the top of the liquid and the lid. Tap the jar lightly on the work surface to remove any air bubbles. Fit the rubber band or metal lid and seal the jar. If using a screw-band jar, loosen by a quarter-turn. Label and store in the refrigerator. Eat within 1 month.

9 If you wish to store the preserve for longer, follow the instructions for bottling on page 23.

EMMA'S TIP Clementines are very simple to prepare but it can take some time! Use a sharp knife so you can remove all the white pith so that the fruits look stunning in the jar.

Fresh Figs in Manuka Honey

Manuka honey from New Zealand is reputed to have anti-bacterial properties. Whether it does or not, its rich, strong flavour complements figs perfectly. Serve this preserve as a dessert with cream or Greek yogurt, or, as they do in Greece, with slices of feta cheese.

MAKES ABOUT: 1L/34FL OZ   **PREPARATION TIME:** 10 MINUTES, PLUS BOTTLING (OPTIONAL)
COOKING TIME: 10 MINUTES

375g/13oz/1⅓ cups Manuka honey
juice of 2 oranges
10 fresh figs

1 Sterilize a 1l/34fl oz preserving jar so that it is ready to use (see page 14).

2 Put the honey and 375ml/13fl oz/1½ cups water in a heavy-based saucepan and heat gently until combined. Bring to the boil and boil for 2 minutes. Remove the pan from the heat.

3 Add the orange juice and figs to the pan. Return the pan to the heat, bring to the boil, then reduce the heat and simmer for 5 minutes until the figs are just tender.

4 Using a slotted spoon, remove the figs from the pan and pack into the warmed, sterilized jar.

5 Pour the remaining liquid over the figs, covering them completely. Leave a 1cm/½in gap between the top of the liquid and the lid. Tap the jar lightly on the work surface to remove any air bubbles. Fit the rubber band or metal lid and seal the jar. If using a screw-band jar, loosen by a quarter-turn. Label and leave to cool completely before storing in the refrigerator. Eat within 1 month.

6 If you wish to store the preserve for longer, follow the instructions for bottling on page 23.

EMMA'S TIP Manuka honey can be expensive but you can use other honeys if you prefer. There are hundreds of varieties to choose from but one from a floral nectar source, such as orange blossom honey, would be a delicious and more affordable alternative.

Tipsy Brandied Fruits

You can choose from a variety of fruits to conserve in brandy, all of which make an excellent dessert. If you want to prepare them as a homemade gift, pack in two smaller preserving jars rather than one large one so that you have one to keep.

MAKES ABOUT: 1L/34FL OZ **PREPARATION TIME:** 40 MINUTES, PLUS 2–3 HOURS COOLING AND 2 WEEKS MATURING, PLUS BOTTLING (OPTIONAL) **COOKING TIME:** 30 MINUTES

750g/1lb 10oz small, firm peaches, apricots or nectarines
375g/13oz/scant 1¾ cups granulated sugar
about 230ml/7¾fl oz/scant 1 cup brandy

1   Bring a large pan of water to the boil. Plunge the fruits individually into the boiling water for 1–2 minutes until their skins split. Remove from the pan using a slotted spoon and use a sharp knife to gently peel off the skin.

2   Sterilize a 1l/34fl oz preserving jar so that it is ready to use (see page 14).

3   Put 150g/5½oz/heaped ⅔ cups of the sugar and 450ml/16fl oz/scant 2 cups water in a heavy-based saucepan and heat gently, stirring until the sugar has dissolved. Add the fruit and simmer gently for 5 minutes, turning, until softened slightly.

4   Using a slotted spoon, remove the fruit from the pan and pack into the warmed, sterilized jar.

5   Add the remaining sugar to the liquid in the pan and heat gently, stirring until dissolved. Bring to the boil and boil until the temperature reaches 110°C/230°F on a sugar thermometer. Turn off the heat and leave until completely cold.

6   Measure the cooled syrup and add an equal quantity of brandy then stir together. Pour the syrup over the fruit, covering it completely. Leave a 1cm/½in gap between the top of the liquid and the lid. Tap the jar lightly on the work surface to remove any air bubbles. Fit the rubber band or metal lid and seal the jar. If using a screw-band jar, loosen by a quarter-turn. Label and store in the refrigerator.

7   Leave to mature for 2 weeks before eating and use within 1 month.

8   If you wish to store the preserve for longer, follow the instructions for bottling on page 23.

EMMA'S TIP Whole fruits look very attractive in jars and make a lovely homemade gift, but sliced fruits take up less space. If you would prefer to use sliced fruit, halve and pit the peaches, apricots or nectarines before putting them in the boiling water.

Cherries in Kirsch

Kirsch is a clear liqueur distilled from cherries and is the perfect choice in which to preserve cherries. Serve spooned over ice cream or use in a Black Forest Gâteau.

MAKES ABOUT: 500ML/17FL OZ **PREPARATION TIME:** 30 MINUTES, PLUS 2–3 HOURS COOLING AND 2 WEEKS MATURING, PLUS BOTTLING (OPTIONAL) **COOKING TIME:** 15 MINUTES

250g/9oz/scant 1¼ cups granulated sugar
500g/1lb 2oz/2½ cups cherries
1 cinnamon stick
about 150ml/5fl oz/scant ⅔ cup kirsch

1 Put 100g/3½oz/scant ½ cup of the sugar and 300ml/10½fl oz/scant 1¼ cups water in a heavy-based saucepan and heat gently, stirring until the sugar has dissolved. Add the cherries and cinnamon stick and gently simmer for 4–5 minutes until the fruit has softened slightly.

2 Drain the cherries and cinnamon stick, reserving the syrup, then return the syrup to the pan.

3 Add the remaining sugar to the pan and heat gently, stirring until dissolved. Bring to the boil and boil until the temperature reaches 110°C/230°F on a sugar thermometer. Leave the syrup for 2–3 hours until completely cold.

4 Sterilize a 500ml/17fl oz preserving jar so that it is ready to use (see page 14).

5 Pack the cherries and cinnamon stick into the warmed, sterilized jar.

6 Measure the cooled syrup and add an equal quantity of kirsch, then stir together. Pour the syrup over the cherries, covering them completely. Leave a 1cm/½in gap between the top of the liquid and the lid. Tap the jar lightly on the work surface to remove any air bubbles. Fit the rubber band or metal lid and seal the jar. If using a screw-band jar, loosen by a quarter-turn. Label and store in the refrigerator.

7 Leave to mature for 2 weeks before eating and use within 1 month.

8 If you wish to store the preserve for longer, follow the instructions for bottling on page 23.

EMMA'S TIP The stones/pits are left in the cherries to help keep their shape; they also impart a pleasant almond flavour to the preserve. However, if you would prefer not to include them, use a sharp knife or a cherry stoner/pitter to pit the cherries before cooking.

Apricots & Chestnuts in Rum

This is a preserve to make during the chestnut season in autumn. Choose plump, smooth nuts, as wrinkled ones have a bitter flavour. Serve as a simple dessert with cream or spoon onto meringues and top with a dollop of thick cream.

MAKES ABOUT: 1L/34FL OZ **PREPARATION TIME:** 40 MINUTES, PLUS 2 WEEKS MATURING, PLUS BOTTLING (OPTIONAL) **COOKING TIME:** 20 MINUTES

350g/12oz/scant 2 cups shelled fresh
   chestnuts
350g/12oz/2 cups dried apricots
400ml/14fl oz/scant 1⅔ cups rum
juice of 1 lemon
juice of 1 orange
300g/10½oz/1⅔ cups granulated sugar

1 Using a sharp knife, nick or snip the brown outer skins off the chestnuts. Put the chestnuts in a saucepan, cover with boiling water and boil for 3–5 minutes. Lift out the chestnuts, a few at a time, and peel off both the outer shell and inner skin.

2 Sterilize a 1l/34fl oz preserving jar so that it is ready to use (see page 14).

3 Put the prepared chestnuts, apricots, rum and 145ml/4¾fl oz/generous ½ cup water in a large heavy-based saucepan. Slowly bring to just below boiling point and simmer for 10 minutes until the chestnuts are tender.

4 Add the lemon juice, orange juice and sugar to the pan. Stir the ingredients together and bring to the boil, then remove the pan from the heat.

5 Using a slotted spoon, remove the chestnuts and apricots from the pan and pack into the warmed, sterilized jar. Pour over the remaining liquid, covering the chestnuts and apricots completely. Leave a 1cm/½in gap between the top of the liquid and the lid. Tap the jar lightly on the work surface to remove any air bubbles. Fit the rubber band or metal lid and seal the jar. If using a screw-band jar, loosen by a quarter-turn. Label and leave to cool completely before storing in the refrigerator.

6 Leave to mature for 2 weeks before eating and use within 1 month.

7 If you wish to store the preserve for longer, follow the instructions for bottling on page 23.

Pears in Mulled Wine

Christmas is the time to serve these pears, when the smell of mulled wine is in the air. Serve as a dessert, and if you have any left over, they are delicious sliced with cold turkey.

MAKES ABOUT: 1L/34FL OZ **PREPARATION TIME:** 25 MINUTES, PLUS BOTTLING (OPTIONAL)
COOKING TIME: 20 MINUTES

1kg/2lb 4oz firm pears, peeled, cored and
    quartered
325ml/11fl oz/scant 1⅔ cups red wine
500g/1lb 2oz/2¼ cups granulated sugar
grated zest and juice of 1 lemon
1 Bay Tree mulled wine spice bundle or
    any other bagged mulling spice mix
1 star anise

1 Put the pears in a saucepan, cover with boiling water and simmer gently for about 5 minutes until almost tender. Drain well.

2 Sterilize a 1l/34fl oz preserving jar so that it is ready to use (see page 14).

3 Put the wine, sugar, lemon zest and juice, mulled wine spice bundle, star anise and 230ml/7¾fl oz/scant 1 cup water in a heavy-based saucepan. Bring to the boil, stirring until the sugar has dissolved, and simmer gently for 5 minutes.

4 Add the pears to the pan and continue to simmer gently for about 5 minutes until the pears are just tender. Test if they are cooked by piercing with a knife. If it goes in easily, they are ready.

5 Using a slotted spoon, remove the pears from the pan and pack into the warmed, sterilized jar. Remove the mulled wine spice bundle from the pan but leave the star anise.

6 Pour the remaining liquid over the pears, covering them completely. Leave a 1cm/½in gap between the top of the liquid and the lid. Tap the jar lightly on the work surface to remove any air bubbles. Fit the rubber band or metal lid and seal the jar. If using a screw-band jar, loosen by a quarter-turn. Label and leave to cool completely before storing in the refrigerator. Eat within 1 month.

7 If you wish to store the preserve for longer, follow the instructions for bottling on page 23.

EMMA'S TIP Mulled wine has been served as a warming winter drink, especially at Christmas and Halloween, for centuries. Originally, spicing wine improved the flavour of good, though poorly stored wines and was not considered a high-class drink. With this in mind, don't choose a delicate-flavoured wine or the cheapest table wine. A fruity, full-bodied red wine that isn't too expensive, such as a Cabernet Sauvignon, Merlot or Shiraz, would be ideal.

Spiced Sherry Plums

These lightly spiced plums are best served as a dessert with a little of the sherry syrup poured over. Add a dollop of thick cream or crème fraîche and serve with small, crisp biscuits or cookies.

MAKES ABOUT: 1L/34FL OZ **PREPARATION TIME:** 55 MINUTES, PLUS 30 MINUTES COOLING AND 2 WEEKS MATURING, PLUS BOTTLING (OPTIONAL) **COOKING TIME:** 10 MINUTES

100g/3½oz/scant ½ cup granulated sugar
800g/1lb 12oz plums
pared zest of 1 orange
1 cinnamon stick
2 star anise
4 whole cloves
270ml/9½fl oz/generous 1 cup
   medium-dry sherry

1 Put the sugar and 230ml/7¾fl oz/scant 1 cup water in a large, heavy-based saucepan and heat gently, stirring until the sugar has dissolved. Bring to the boil and boil for 1 minute. Remove from the heat and stir in a further 200ml/7fl oz/scant 1 cup water.

2 If you like, halve and pit the plums (reserving a few pits for later) or leave them whole. Add the plums (skin-side down if halved), orange zest, cinnamon stick, star anise and cloves to the pan and simmer gently for 4–5 minutes until the plum skins split. If using whole plums, turn once or twice in the liquid.

3 Drain the plums and spices, reserving the syrup. Leave the syrup to cool.

4 Using a sharp knife, gently peel the skins from the plums. Discard the skins and leave the plums to cool.

5 Sterilize a 1l/34fl oz preserving jar so that it is ready to use (see page 14).

6 Pack the cooled plums and spices into the warmed, sterilized jar. If you like, you can add a few of the reserved pits to the jar to impart their almond flavour.

7 Add the sherry to the cooled syrup, stir, and then pour the syrup over the plums, covering them completely. Leave a 1cm/½in gap between the top of the liquid and the lid. Tap the jar lightly on the work surface to remove any air bubbles. Fit the rubber band or metal lid and seal the jar. If using a screw-band jar, loosen by a quarter-turn. Label and store in the refrigerator.

8 Leave to mature for 2 weeks before eating and use within 1 month.

9 If you wish to store the preserve for longer, follow the instructions for bottling on page 23.

Dark Chocolate Sauce

Rich and thick, this is for real chocolate lovers. It can't be kept for a long time, but it is unlikely that you will need to! Serve it hot or cold, drizzled over vanilla ice cream, chocolate brownies, strawberries, profiteroles or chocolate cake, or sneak a spoonful from the jar.

MAKES ABOUT: 250ML/9FL OZ **PREPARATION TIME:** 5 MINUTES **COOKING TIME:** 10 MINUTES

115g/4oz unsalted butter, cut into pieces
450g/1lb dark/bittersweet chocolate
  (minimum 70% cocoa solids),
  broken into pieces
230ml/7¾fl oz/scant 1 cup
  double/heavy cream

1 Sterilize enough wide-necked jars in the oven so that they are ready to use (see page 14).
2 Put the butter and chocolate in a heatproof bowl over a saucepan of gently simmering water, making sure the bottom of the bowl does not touch the water. Heat gently, stirring the mixture until the butter and chocolate has melted and the mixture has combined.
3 Gradually stir in the cream until the sauce is smooth.
4 The sauce can be used immediately and served hot. Alternatively, to store, pour into the warmed, sterilized jars, seal immediately and label. Leave to cool completely before storing in the refrigerator for up to 3 weeks.
5 Serve cold or, to serve hot, reheat the sauce gently in a saucepan.

EMMA'S TIP Dark Chocolate Sauce and Butterscotch Sauce freeze well, if you make more than you need. Pour into a plastic container, leave to cool and then seal and store in the freezer. Leave to thaw at room temperature for about 8 hours before serving. Keep in the refrigerator once opened.

Butterscotch Sauce

Serve this luxurious, traditional sauce poured over ice cream, hot puddings, gingerbread, pancakes and any other of your favourite desserts. Butterscotch sauce doesn't have a long preserving life but, if you have any left over, you can freeze it and keep to serve with ice cream for a quick dessert.

MAKES ABOUT: 250ML/9FL OZ **PREPARATION TIME:** 5 MINUTES **COOKING TIME:** 10 MINUTES

125g/4½oz unsalted butter, cut into pieces
125g/4½oz/⅔ cup soft light brown sugar
125g/4½oz golden syrup/light corn syrup
½ tsp vanilla extract

1 Sterilize enough wide-necked jars in the oven so that they are ready to use (see page 14).

2 Put the butter, sugar, golden syrup and vanilla extract in a heatproof bowl over a saucepan of gently simmering water. Heat gently, stirring until the butter has melted, the sugar has dissolved, the ingredients are combined and the sauce is smooth.

3 The sauce can be used immediately and served hot. Alternatively, to store, pour into the warmed, sterilized jars, seal immediately and label. Leave to cool completely before storing in the refrigerator for up to 3 weeks.

4 Serve cold or, to serve hot, reheat the sauce gently in a saucepan.

Elderflower Cordial

Early summer is the time to make this cordial, when you will see elder shrubs and trees covered in pretty white flowers. Collect the flowers when just in bloom and use while very fresh so they retain their fragrant perfume. Elderflower cordial is delicious with sparkling water and Prosecco, and can also be added to fruit salads, fools and crumbles. It particularly complements gooseberries.

MAKES ABOUT: 1.5L/52FL OZ **PREPARATION TIME:** 20 MINUTES, PLUS 24 HOURS INFUSING
COOKING TIME: 5 MINUTES

**175g/6oz elderflower heads
 (about 25 large heads)
pared zest and juice of 2 lemons
900g/2lb/heaped 4 cups granulated sugar**

1 Remove any insects from the elderflower heads (there is no need to wash the flowers). Put the elderflowers and lemon zest in a bowl and add 1.5l/52fl oz/6 cups water. Cover and leave to infuse in a cool place for 24 hours, stirring occasionally as you pass.

2 The next day, strain the liquid into a preserving pan. Add the lemon juice and sugar to the pan and heat gently, stirring until the sugar has dissolved, then simmer for 2–3 minutes.

3 Strain the liquid through a piece of muslin/cheesecloth.

4 To store, pour the cordial into clean plastic bottles, leaving 2.5cm/1in space at the top to allow for expansion. Label and freeze (see tip below) until fully frozen.

5 Thaw the cordial at room temperature for about 8 hours. To serve as a drink, dilute to taste with still or sparking water. Keep in the refrigerator once opened and use within 2 days.

EMMA'S TIP Elderflower cordial recipes often contain citric acid, which is needed to create an acidic environment to stop the fermentation process. Unfortunately, few chemists sell it now; the solution is to freeze the cordial as suggested in the recipe. Freeze in plastic bottles to allow for expansion, but you could transfer to glass bottles when thawed if you prefer.

Old-Fashioned Lemonade

This traditional sweet and sour drink is popular with adults and children; perhaps it is nostalgia and the thought of long summers spent lazily in the sunshine as a child. It is certainly far superior to any commercial product you can buy. Tastes have changed over the years, and archive recipes use fewer lemons and more sugar. You can adjust the taste to your liking by adding more lemon juice or sugar before storing.

MAKES ABOUT: 1.5L/52FL OZ **PREPARATION TIME:** 20 MINUTES, PLUS 12 HOURS OR OVERNIGHT INFUSING
COOKING TIME: 10 MINUTES

6 lemons
150g/5½oz/heaped ⅔ cup granulated sugar
lemon slices and mint sprigs, to serve

1 Using a potato peeler, thinly pare the zest from the lemons. Do not include any pith or it will make the lemonade taste bitter.

2 Put the lemon zest, sugar and 1.45l/50fl oz/ 5¾ cups water in a large saucepan and slowly bring to the boil, stirring to dissolve the sugar. Reduce the heat and simmer for 5 minutes.

3 Pour the syrup into a large bowl or jug/pitcher, cover and leave to infuse for 12 hours or overnight in a cool place.

4 The next day, squeeze the juice from the lemons. Strain the cooled syrup through a sieve into a clean large bowl or jug. Add the lemon juice and stir together.

5 To store, pour the lemonade into clean plastic bottles, leaving 2.5cm/1in to allow for expansion. Label and freeze (see the tip box on page 115) until fully frozen.

6 Thaw at room temperature for about 8 hours and then serve chilled with lemon slices and mint sprigs. Keep in the refrigerator once opened and use within 2 days.

Crème de Cassis

This blackcurrant liqueur is what you use to make the French apéritif kir. Pour a splash of crème de cassis into a glass and top up with white wine. There is also Kir Royale, made with Champagne; Kir Pétillant, made with sparkling wine; Kir Normand, made with Normandy cider; and Kir Breton, made with Breton cider. Two other liqueurs that can be made in the same way are crème de framboise, with raspberries, and crème de mûre, with blackberries.

MAKES ABOUT: 1.5L/52FL OZ **PREPARATION TIME:** 35 MINUTES, PLUS 8 WEEKS MACERATING, AND 48 HOURS AND 6 MONTHS MATURING

1kg/2lb 4oz/8⅓ cups blackcurrants, stripped
1l/34fl oz/4 cups brandy, gin or vodka
175g/6oz/heaped ¾ cup granulated sugar per
**   600ml/21fl oz/scant 2½ cups of liquid**

1 Sterilize a large enough jar that will hold the blackcurrants and spirit (see page 14).

2 Put the blackcurrants in a bowl and crush with a fork. Put into the sterilized jar and pour in the spirit. Cover with a tight-fitting lid and leave the jar in a cool, dark place for 8 weeks.

3 After the blackcurrants have macerated, strain the mixture through a sieve into a large jug/pitcher.

4 Measure the liquid and for each 600ml/21fl oz/ scant 2½ cups of liquid, add 175g/6oz/heaped ¾ cup sugar.

5 Pour the mixture into a large jug or bowl, cover and leave at room temperature for 48 hours, stirring occasionally as you pass to dissolve the sugar.

6 Sterilize enough bottles so that they are ready to use (see page 14).

7 Line a sieve with muslin/cheesecloth and strain the mixture. Pour the liqueur into the sterilized bottles, seal and label.

8 Store the liqueur in a cool, dry, dark place for 6 months before using.

EMMA'S TIP To strip blackcurrants easily from their stalks, hold each stalk at the top of the bunch over a bowl and run a fork firmly down the stem. The blackcurrants should then come away easily.

Limoncello

This is a wonderful homemade version of the sweet, lemony Italian liqueur. Serve it as they do in Italy, either before a meal or afterwards, in small glasses poured over ice cubes. Alternatively, drizzle over vanilla ice cream or strawberries.

MAKES ABOUT: 1.5L/52FL OZ **PREPARATION TIME:** 35 MINUTES, PLUS 2–3 HOURS COOLING, 10 DAYS MACERATING AND 10 DAYS INFUSING **COOKING TIME:** 5 MINUTES

6 lemons
1l/34fl oz/4 cups vodka
500g/1lb 2oz/2¼ cups granulated sugar

1 Sterilize a 1l/34fl oz jar so that it is ready to use (see page 14).

2 Using a potato peeler, thinly pare the zest from the lemons. Do not include any pith or it will make the Limoncello taste bitter.

3 Put the lemon zest in the warmed, sterilized jar and pour in the vodka. Cover with a tight-fitting lid and leave the jar in a light place at room temperature for at least 10 days. Tip the jar once a day to agitate the zest.

4 After the lemon zest has macerated, put the sugar and 500ml/17fl oz/2 cups water in a large saucepan and slowly bring to the boil, stirring to dissolve the sugar. Reduce the heat and simmer for 5 minutes. Remove from the heat and leave for 2–3 hours until completely cold.

5 Add the lemon zest and vodka mixture to the cooled syrup and stir together.

6 Sterilize 1 large or several small jars. Pour the mixture into the jars and leave to infuse for a further 10 days to allow the flavours to develop. This time there is no need to shake the jar(s).

7 Sterilize enough freezerproof plastic or glass bottles so that they are ready to use (see page 14).

8 Line a sieve with muslin/cheesecloth and strain the mixture. Pour the Limoncello into the sterilized bottles. Seal and label. Store the bottles in the freezer.

EMMA'S TIP It is safe to store glass bottles of Limoncello in the freezer, as vodka does not freeze in domestic freezers, so will not expand.

Sloe Gin

Sloes can be found in hedgerows in the autumn, but the best time to collect them is when the first frosts have arrived. The frost breaks down the sloes, which helps to release their juices and flavour. You can gather sloes earlier and put them in the freezer to get the same effect; this may mean you get to the sloes before the birds do, too!

MAKES ABOUT: 1L/34FL OZ **PREPARATION TIME:** 45 MINUTES, PLUS 11 WEEKS MACERATING AND 12 MONTHS MATURING (OPTIONAL)

500g/1lb 2oz/3¼ cups sloes
350g/12oz/scant 1⅔ cups granulated sugar
750ml/26fl oz/3 cups gin

1 Sterilize enough jars that the sloes will half fill so that they are ready to use (see page 14).
2 If the sloes haven't been affected by the frost or you have not frozen them, prick each sloe several times with a sewing needle.
3 Half-fill the warmed, sterilized jars with the sloes. Divide the sugar equally among the jars and pour over the gin. Cover with tight-fitting lids and shake the jars well.
4 Leave the jars in a cool, dry, dark place. Shake once a day for 1 week and then once a week for 10 weeks.

5 Sterilize enough bottles so that they are ready to use (see page 14).
6 Line a sieve with muslin/cheesecloth and strain the mixture. Pour the strained liqueur into the sterilized bottles, seal and label. Store in a cool, dry, dark place. The liqueur can be drunk immediately but ideally should be stored for 1 year before drinking.

Chutneys & Relishes

Pear & Ginger Chutney

A sweet and spicy chutney and, if you like ginger, you will find it difficult to resist another spoonful! It gets even better as it matures and is particularly good served with pork, as an accompaniment to curry or with cold meats, cheese and bread.

MAKES ABOUT: 1.5KG/3LB 5OZ **PREPARATION TIME:** 35 MINUTES, PLUS 1 MONTH MATURING
COOKING TIME: 2 HOURS 5 MINUTES

600ml/21fl oz/scant 2½ cups red wine vinegar
2kg/4lb 8oz pears, peeled,
    cored and chopped
20g/¾oz fresh ginger, peeled
    and finely chopped
70g/2½oz stem/preserved ginger,
    finely chopped
350g/12oz onions, chopped
500g/1lb 2oz/2¼ cups granulated sugar
grated zest and juice of 2 oranges
½ tsp ground cloves

1 Pour the vinegar into a preserving pan. Add all the remaining ingredients, stir together and slowly bring to the boil.

2 Reduce the heat and simmer for about 2 hours or until no excess liquid remains and the mixture is thick. Stir from time to time to prevent the mixture from sticking to the bottom of the pan.

3 Meanwhile, sterilize enough jars with non-metallic, vinegar-proof lids, or preserving jars, so that they are ready to use (see page 14).

4 Spoon the chutney into the warmed, sterilized jars. Seal immediately, label and store in a cool, dry, dark place.

5 Leave to mature for at least 1 month before using. Refrigerate after opening.

Flaming Mango Chutney

This spicy, fresh-tasting Indian chutney is the perfect addition to any curry, particularly a lamb or chicken-based recipe. It is also delicious simply scooped up with poppadoms, parathas or chapatis.

MAKES ABOUT: 1.3KG/3LB **PREPARATION TIME**: 35 MINUTES, PLUS 1 MONTH MATURING
COOKING TIME: 1¼ HOURS

300ml/10½fl oz/scant 1¼ cups
   white wine vinegar
⅓ red bird's eye chilli, finely chopped,
   seeds reserved
4 garlic cloves, finely chopped
500g/1lb 2oz/2¼ cups Demerara sugar
25g/1oz garlic paste
3 tbsp ground cumin
2½ tsp salt
2 mangoes, pitted, peeled and
   roughly chopped

1 Pour the vinegar into a preserving pan. Add all the remaining ingredients, except the mangoes, and slowly bring to the boil. Add the chilli seeds if you like a hot flavour.

2 Reduce the heat and boil gently for about 10 minutes, stirring occasionally, until the mixture is reduced by a third.

3 Add the mangoes to the pan and simmer gently for 1 hour until the mango has softened but still holds its shape and there is no excess liquid in the pan. Stir from time to time to prevent the mixture from sticking to the bottom of the pan.

4 Meanwhile, sterilize enough jars with non-metallic, vinegar-proof lids, or preserving jars, so that they are ready to use (see page 14).

5 Spoon the chutney into the warmed, sterilized jars. Seal immediately, label and store in a cool, dry, dark place.

6 Leave to mature for at least 1 month before using. Refrigerate after opening.

Gingered Plum Chutney

Flavoured with ginger and allspice (a spice in its own right that tastes like cloves, cinnamon and nutmeg) this chutney is perfect to serve with crusty bread and cheese. Dry, sharp cheeses, such as feta and goats' cheese, work particularly well, as they contrast with the sweetness of the chutney.

MAKES ABOUT: 950G/2LB 2OZ **PREPARATION TIME:** 30 MINUTES, PLUS 1 MONTH MATURING
COOKING TIME: 1 HOUR 20 MINUTES

230ml/7¾fl oz/scant 1 cup red wine vinegar
1kg/2lb 4oz plums, halved, pitted
    and chopped
500g/1lb 2oz cooking apples, peeled,
    cored and chopped
360g/12¾oz/scant 2 cups
    soft light brown sugar
20g/¾oz ginger paste
1 tbsp ground allspice

1 Pour the vinegar into a preserving pan. Add all the remaining ingredients, stir together and slowly bring to the boil.

2 Reduce the heat and simmer gently for about 1¼ hours until the mixture is light brown and thick. Stir occasionally to prevent the mixture from sticking to the bottom of the pan.

3 Meanwhile, sterilize enough jars with non-metallic, vinegar-proof lids, or preserving jars, so that they are ready to use (see page 14).

4 Spoon the chutney into the warmed, sterilized jars. Seal immediately, label and store in a cool, dry, dark place.

5 Leave to mature for at least 1 month before using. Refrigerate after opening.

Spicy Rhubarb & Orange Chutney

There is more to do with rhubarb than putting it in a crumble! This mildly spiced chutney complements smoked mackerel, cold ham or hot gammon steaks. It is also delicious served with a cheeseboard.

MAKES ABOUT: 1.3KG/3LB **PREPARATION TIME:** 35 MINUTES, PLUS 1 MONTH MATURING
COOKING TIME: 1 HOUR 35 MINUTES

400ml/14fl oz/scant 1⅔ cups red wine vinegar
400g/14oz/scant 2¼ cups
    soft light brown sugar
1kg/2lb 4oz pink rhubarb, chopped
1kg/2lb 4oz red onions, finely chopped
6 garlic cloves, finely chopped
200g/7oz tomatoes, chopped
grated zest and juice of 4 oranges
2 tsp ground ginger
1 tsp ground cinnamon
¼ tsp ground cloves

1 Put the vinegar, sugar and 125ml/4fl oz/½ cup water in a preserving pan and slowly bring to the boil, stirring until the sugar has dissolved.

2 Add the rhubarb, onions, garlic, tomatoes, orange juice, ginger, cinnamon and cloves to the pan. Reduce the heat and simmer gently for about 1½ hours or until no excess liquid remains and the mixture is thick. Stir from time to time to prevent the mixture from sticking to the bottom of the pan.

3 Meanwhile, sterilize enough jars with non-metallic, vinegar-proof lids, or preserving jars, so that they are ready to use (see page 14).

4 Add the orange zest to the pan and stir everything together.

5 Spoon the chutney into the warmed, sterilized jars. Seal immediately, label and store in a cool, dry, dark place.

6 Leave to mature for at least 1 month before using. Refrigerate after opening.

Indian Lime Chutney

Often referred to as a pickle but actually a chutney, this tangy preserve goes well with Indian curries but also with Middle Eastern foods such as lamb and couscous.

MAKES ABOUT: 800G/1LB 12OZ **PREPARATION TIME:** 30 MINUTES, PLUS 48 HOURS CURING AND 1 MONTH MATURING **COOKING TIME:** 1½–2 HOURS

6 limes
6 tbsp coarse salt
4 tbsp rapeseed/canola oil
2 tsp mustard seeds
4 garlic cloves, finely chopped
2 tsp ginger paste
½ tsp chilli powder
1 tsp mustard powder
2 tsp ground fenugreek
2 tsp paprika
1 tsp ground turmeric
300ml/10½fl oz/scant 1¼ cups
    distilled white vinegar
250g/9oz/scant 1¼ cups Demerara sugar

1 Cut the limes into eighths and then cut each eighth into 4 pieces. Discard the seeds. Put the lime pieces in a large bowl and sprinkle over the salt. Cover the bowl and leave to cure in a cool place for 48 hours, stirring occasionally.

2 Drain the limes, rinse well under cold running water and drain.

3 Heat the oil in a large, heavy-based saucepan. Add the mustard seeds and cook for 30 seconds, or until they start to jump in the pan (be careful as they can burn you). Add the garlic, ginger paste, chilli powder, mustard powder, fenugreek, paprika and turmeric and cook for 30 seconds to allow the spices to release their flavour.

4 Add the vinegar and lime pieces to the pan, return to the boil, then reduce the heat and simmer gently for 1 hour. Stir occasionally to prevent the mixture from sticking to the bottom of the pan.

5 Add the sugar to the pan and slowly bring to the boil, stirring until the sugar has dissolved. Reduce the heat and simmer gently for 5 minutes, stirring all the time. Be very careful towards the end of cooking that the chutney does not become too thick, as it thickens further as it cools.

6 Meanwhile, sterilize enough jars with non-metallic, vinegar-proof lids, or preserving jars, so that they are ready to use (see page 14).

7 Spoon the chutney into the warmed, sterilized jars. Seal immediately, label and store in a cool, dry, dark place.

8 Leave to mature for at least 1 month before using. Refrigerate after opening.

Curried Apricot & Apple Chutney

This chutney has several uses and it goes particularly well with chicken. Serve as an accompaniment to cold chicken, or add a spoonful to yogurt and use as a dressing for a chicken salad, or to mayonnaise to make Coronation Chicken. Alternatively, add to a stuffing mix to serve with roast chicken.

MAKES ABOUT: 1.25KG/2LB 12OZ **PREPARATION TIME:** 35 MINUTES, PLUS 1 MONTH MATURING
COOKING TIME: 50 MINUTES

200ml/7fl oz/scant 1 cup coconut milk
1½ tsp curry powder
¾ tsp ginger paste
185ml/6fl oz/¾ cup apple cider vinegar
175g/6oz onions, chopped
500g/1lb 2oz/2¾ cups dried apricots, chopped
425g/15oz cooking apples, peeled, cored and chopped
150g/5½oz/heaped ⅔ cup granulated sugar

1 Put the coconut milk in a jug/pitcher, add the curry powder and ginger paste and mix together.

2 Put the curried coconut milk and vinegar in a preserving pan. Add the onions, apricots, apples and sugar, stir together and slowly bring to the boil.

3 Reduce the heat and simmer gently for about 45 minutes until the onions and apricots are soft and no excess liquid remains. Do not allow the mixture to get too thick. Stir regularly to prevent the mixture from sticking to the bottom of the pan.

4 Meanwhile, sterilize enough jars with non-metallic, vinegar-proof lids, or preserving jars, so that they are ready to use (see page 14).

5 Spoon the chutney into the warmed, sterilized jars. Seal immediately, label and store in a cool, dry, dark place.

6 Leave to mature for at least 1 month before using. Refrigerate after opening.

EMMA'S TIP Use yellow dried apricots if you can find them, rather than ready-to-eat or brown dried apricots, as the colour is much better for this preserve.

Apricot & Walnut Chutney

This uncomplicated recipe makes a light, fresh chutney with the additional crunch of chopped walnuts. It is the perfect addition to a cheeseboard or a lamb, pork or poultry dish, whether the meat is served hot or cold.

MAKES ABOUT: 1.7KG/3LB 12OZ   **PREPARATION TIME:** 30 MINUTES, PLUS 1 MONTH MATURING
COOKING TIME: 1½ HOURS

400ml/14fl oz/scant 1⅔ cups
   apple cider vinegar
1kg/2lb 4oz apricots, pitted and chopped
500g/1lb 2oz red onions, finely chopped
40g/1½oz fresh ginger, peeled and
   finely chopped
200g/7oz/scant 1⅔ cups
   sultanas/golden raisins
500g/1lb 2oz/2¼ cups Demerara sugar
grated zest and juice of 1 orange
½ tsp ground cinnamon
1 tsp salt
150g/5½oz/1½ cups walnuts, chopped

1 Pour the vinegar and 200ml/7fl oz/scant 1 cup water into a preserving pan. Add the remaining ingredients, stir together and slowly bring to the boil.

2 Reduce the heat and simmer for about 1½ hours until no excess liquid remains and the mixture is thick. Stir from time to time to prevent the mixture from sticking to the bottom of the pan.

3 Meanwhile, sterilize enough jars with non-metallic, vinegar-proof lids, or preserving jars, so that they are ready to use (see page 14).

4 Spoon the chutney into the warmed, sterilized jars. Seal immediately, label and store in a cool, dry, dark place.

5 Leave to mature for at least 1 month before using. Refrigerate after opening.

EMMA'S TIP You can make variations of this recipe by replacing the apricots with peaches or nectarines and the walnuts with pecan nuts. You can also use dried apricots as opposed to fresh and, if you choose these, you will need 700g/1lb 9oz, which should be soaked in water for 12 hours and then drained (or use ready-to-eat dried apricots).

Banana & Date Chutney

Like most chutneys, this is an excellent accompaniment to curries, particularly spicy chicken recipes. It also goes well with cold turkey and chicken, as the sweetness of the fruits enhances the taste of the poultry.

MAKES ABOUT: 1.7KG/3LB 12OZ **PREPARATION TIME:** 35 MINUTES, PLUS 1 MONTH MATURING
COOKING TIME: 40 MINUTES

½ tsp cumin seeds
500ml/17fl oz/2 cups apple cider vinegar
1.25kg/2lb 12oz bananas, peeled and sliced
250g/9oz/heaped 1⅓ cups fresh or dried
　dates, halved and pitted
250g/9oz onions, chopped
325g/11½oz/1½ cups granulated sugar
1 tsp ginger paste
½ tsp chilli powder
1½ tsp ground mace
½ tsp salt
grated zest and juice of 1 orange

1　Put the cumin seeds in a non-stick frying pan and dry-fry, tossing continuously, for about 1 minute until golden brown.

2　Pour the vinegar and 500ml/17fl oz/2 cups water into a preserving pan. Add the remaining ingredients, except the orange zest and juice, stir together and slowly bring to the boil.

3　Reduce the heat and simmer gently for about 30 minutes until the onions are soft and only a little liquid remains on the surface. Do not allow the mixture to get too thick and dark. Stir regularly to mix the ingredients and prevent the mixture from sticking to the bottom of the pan.

4　Meanwhile, sterilize enough jars with non-metallic, vinegar-proof lids, or preserving jars, so that they are ready to use (see page 14).

5　Stir the orange zest and juice into the cooked chutney and simmer for a further 5 minutes.

6　Spoon the chutney into the warmed, sterilized jars. Seal immediately, label and store in a cool, dry, dark place.

7　Leave to mature for at least 1 month before using. Refrigerate after opening.

Green Tomato Chutney

An old favourite, just like your grandmother used to make. If you have any unripened tomatoes at the end of the season, this is the classic recipe to use them up. Use the chutney to enhance any dish, and it is delicious in sandwiches, of course.

MAKES ABOUT: 1.25KG/2LB 12OZ **PREPARATION TIME:** 40 MINUTES, PLUS 1 MONTH MATURING
COOKING TIME: 1 HOUR 35 MINUTES

2 tsp pickling spice
425ml/15fl oz/generous 1⅔ cups
   distilled white vinegar
500g/1lb 2oz green tomatoes, chopped
500g/1lb 2oz cooking apples, peeled,
   cored and chopped
400g/14oz onions, chopped
200g/7oz/scant 1⅔ cups raisins
400g/14oz/heaped 1¾ cups Demerara sugar
1 garlic clove, chopped
½ tsp cayenne pepper
1 tsp ground ginger
1 tsp salt

1 Tie the pickling spice in a piece of muslin/ cheesecloth.

2 Pour the vinegar into a preserving pan. Add the muslin bag and all the remaining ingredients, stir together and slowly bring to the boil.

3 Reduce the heat and simmer for about 1½ hours or until the mixture is dark and thick and only a little liquid remains on the surface. Do not allow the mixture to get too thick. Stir regularly to prevent the mixture from sticking to the bottom of the pan.

4 Meanwhile, sterilize enough jars with non-metallic, vinegar-proof lids, or preserving jars, so that they are ready to use (see page 14).

5 Spoon the chutney into the warmed, sterilized jars. Seal immediately, label and store in a cool, dry, dark place.

6 Leave to mature for at least 1 month before using. Refrigerate after opening.

EMMA'S TIP If you would like to make your own pickling spice, combine equal quantities of coriander seeds, yellow mustard seeds and whole allspice in a jar and add a few whole cloves and peppercorns. Use as required, adding a bay leaf and cinnamon stick before cooking. You need 25g/1oz for every 1l/34fl oz/4 cups vinegar.

Carrot & Date Chutney

The texture of this chutney is slightly crunchy and, apart from serving it with cheese and cold meats, it would make a good addition to a stuffing mix. An alternative suggestion is to spread it inside small pita breads, top with thin slices of chicken or lamb and serve with minted yogurt and a wedge of lime.

MAKES ABOUT: 1.5KG/3LB 5OZ **PREPARATION TIME:** 35 MINUTES, PLUS 1 MONTH MATURING
COOKING TIME: 1 HOUR

10g/¼oz pickling spice
400ml/14fl oz/scant 1⅔ cups
   apple cider vinegar
300g/10½oz onions, finely chopped
500g/1lb 2oz carrots, grated
425g/15oz/2⅓ cups pitted dried dates,
   chopped
250g/9oz/scant 1¼ cups granulated sugar

1 Tie the pickling spice in a piece of muslin/cheesecloth.

2 Pour the vinegar and 1l/34fl oz/4 cups water into a preserving pan. Add the muslin bag, onions, carrots, dates and sugar, stir together and slowly bring to the boil.

3 Reduce the heat and simmer for about 1 hour or until no excess liquid remains. Do not allow the mixture to get too thick. Stir regularly to prevent the mixture from sticking to the bottom of the pan.

4 Meanwhile, sterilize enough jars with non-metallic, vinegar-proof lids, or preserving jars, so that they are ready to use (see page 14).

5 Spoon the chutney into the warmed, sterilized jars. Seal immediately, label and store in a cool, dry, dark place.

6 Leave to mature for at least 1 month before using. Refrigerate after opening.

EMMA'S TIP The recipe suggests using pitted, dried dates but fresh dates can also be used. Remove the stones first; slit each date open lengthways and push the stone out with your fingers.

Indian Tomato & Nigella Seed Chutney

Nigella seeds are sometimes referred to as black onion or black cumin seeds, but they are not connected to either and are the seeds of *Nigella sativa*, an annual flowering herb. This sweet chutney is a delicious accompaniment to serve with your favourite curry.

MAKES ABOUT: 950G/2LB 2OZ **PREPARATION TIME:** 40 MINUTES **COOKING TIME:** 1 HOUR 35 MINUTES

2kg/4lb 8oz tomatoes
600ml/21fl oz/scant 2½ cups
   distilled white vinegar
1kg/2lb 2oz/4½ cups granulated sugar
8 garlic cloves, crushed
4 tsp nigella seeds
100g/3½oz/heaped ¾ cup raisins
50g/1¾oz/⅓ cup blanched almonds, chopped
1 tsp dried chilli flakes
3 bay leaves
1 tsp salt

1 With a sharp knife, cut a cross in the skin of each tomato, then put into a heatproof bowl and cover with boiling water. Leave to stand for 2–3 minutes, then drain. Peel off and discard the skins. Roughly chop the flesh.

2 Put the tomatoes, vinegar and 300ml/10½fl oz/ scant 1¼ cups water in a preserving pan. Add all the remaining ingredients, stir together and slowly bring to the boil.

3 Reduce the heat and simmer for about 1½ hours until no excess liquid remains. Stir from time to time to prevent the mixture from sticking to the bottom of the pan. Remove and discard the bay leaves.

4 Meanwhile, sterilize enough jars with non-metallic, vinegar-proof lids, or preserving jars, so that they are ready to use (see page 14).

5 Spoon the chutney into the warmed, sterilized jars. Seal immediately and label. The chutney can be eaten immediately and doesn't need to mature. Refrigerate after opening.

Beetroot & Orange Chutney

This is a chutney for beetroot lovers. Lightly spiced and a wonderful vivid, ruby red colour, it is best served with pork or cheese, particularly goats' cheese or a tasty mature Cheddar. If you have a little over when you come to putting it in the jars, save it to serve warm with, for example, roast pork, grilled sausages or a beef stew.

MAKES ABOUT: 1.7KG/3LB 12OZ **PREPARATION TIME:** 40 MINUTES, PLUS 1 MONTH MATURING
COOKING TIME: 2½ HOURS

500ml/17fl oz/2 cups red wine vinegar
1kg/2lb 4oz raw beetroot/beet, peeled
    and diced
750g/1lb 10oz cooking apples, peeled,
    cored and chopped
350g/12oz onions, chopped
500g/1lb 2oz/2¼ cups granulated sugar
1 tsp grated nutmeg
1 tsp mixed spice/pumpkin pie spice
1½ tsp ground cloves
grated zest and juice of 1 orange

1 Pour the vinegar into a preserving pan. Add all the remaining ingredients, except the orange zest and juice, stir together and slowly bring to the boil.

2 Reduce the heat and simmer for about 2¼ hours until the mixture is thick and only a little liquid remains on the surface. Stir occasionally to prevent the mixture from sticking to the bottom of the pan.

3 Meanwhile, sterilize enough jars with non-metallic, vinegar-proof lids, or preserving jars, so that they are ready to use (see page 14).

4 Stir the orange zest and juice into the pan. Increase the heat and cook for about 5 minutes until only a little liquid remains on the surface. Do not allow the mixture to get too dark. Stir regularly to prevent the mixture from sticking to the bottom of the pan.

5 Spoon the chutney into the warmed, sterilized jars. Seal immediately, label and store in a cool, dry, dark place.

6 Leave to mature for at least 1 month before using. Refrigerate after opening.

EMMA'S TIP Beetroot juices stain so if you want to avoid bright red hands, wear protective rubber or disposable gloves when preparing it and use a plastic chopping board rather than a wooden one. Alternatively, you could use golden beetroot; it has a more subtle flavour than red beetroot but also has a beautiful, vibrant colour that doesn't stain.

Cool Chilli & Apple Chutney

If you like something with just a little heat (hence its name), this spicy apple chutney is the perfect partner for cheese and cold meats. It also works very well served with roast pork as an alternative to apple sauce.

MAKES ABOUT: 1KG/2LB 4OZ **PREPARATION TIME:** 35 MINUTES, PLUS 1 MONTH MATURING
COOKING TIME: 1 HOUR 35 MINUTES

450ml/16fl oz/scant 2 cups
   apple cider vinegar
1kg/2lb 4oz eating apples, peeled,
   cored and chopped
300g/10½oz onions, chopped
400g/14oz/heaped 1¾ cups Demerara sugar
200g/7oz red peppers, halved lengthways,
   deseeded and chopped
1 tsp dried chilli flakes
2 tbsp peeled and grated fresh ginger
½ tsp grated nutmeg
½ tsp ground allspice
¼ tsp ground cloves
2 tsp salt

1 Pour the vinegar and 450ml/16fl oz/scant 2 cups water into a preserving pan. Add the remaining ingredients, stir together and slowly bring to the boil.

2 Reduce the heat and simmer for 1½ hours or until no excess liquid remains and the mixture is thick. Stir from time to time to prevent the mixture from sticking to the bottom of the pan.

3 Meanwhile, sterilize enough jars with non-metallic, vinegar-proof lids, or preserving jars, so that they are ready to use (see page 14).

4 Spoon the chutney into the warmed, sterilized jars. Seal immediately, label and store in a cool, dry, dark place.

5 Leave to mature for at least 1 month before using. Refrigerate after opening.

Fig & Balsamic Relish

With its sweet and sour flavour, this distinctive relish is best served with cold meats or chicken liver pâté or cheese, particularly a salty sheep's or tangy goats' cheese. The recipe suggests using dried figs, as they are less expensive and readily available, but you could use 20–22 fresh figs instead if you have a bumper harvest.

MAKES ABOUT: 1.8KG/4LB **PREPARATION TIME:** 40 MINUTES, PLUS 1 MONTH MATURING
COOKING TIME: 55 MINUTES

1 tbsp olive oil
500g/1lb 2oz red onions, sliced
250g/9oz cooking apples, peeled,
　cored and chopped
150ml/5fl oz/scant ⅔ cup balsamic vinegar
85ml/2¾fl oz/⅓ cup sherry vinegar
1 tsp ginger paste
500g/1lb 2oz dried figs, roughly chopped
150g/5½oz dried apricots, roughly chopped
grated zest and juice of 2 oranges
¾ tsp salt

1　Heat the oil in a preserving pan. Add the onions and fry gently for about 15 minutes until softened and beginning to turn brown.

2　Add the apples, balsamic vinegar, sherry vinegar, ginger paste and 500ml/17fl oz/2 cups water to the pan. Bring to the boil, then reduce the heat and simmer for 15 minutes, stirring occasionally, until the onions are soft.

3　Add the figs, apricots, orange juice and salt to the pan and continue to simmer gently for about 20 minutes until only a little liquid remains in the bottom of the pan and the mixture is soft and combined but not too thick. Stir occasionally to prevent the mixture from sticking to the bottom of the pan.

4　Meanwhile, sterilize enough jars with non-metallic, vinegar-proof lids, or preserving jars, so that they are ready to use (see page 14).

5　Add the orange zest to the pan and stir everything together.

6　Spoon the relish into the warmed, sterilized jars. Seal immediately, label and store in a cool, dry, dark place.

7　Leave to mature for at least 1 month before using. Refrigerate after opening.

EMMA'S TIP When chopping dried figs, dip the knife into hot water occasionally as this helps to stop them from sticking to the knife.

Beetroot & Horseradish Relish

The beetroot is crunchy and sweet with just a minor kick added by the horseradish. It is a relish that is excellent as a cold accompaniment with smoked fish, cold meats or cheese. You can also warm it to serve with roast beef.

MAKES ABOUT: 1.25KG/2LB 12OZ **PREPARATION TIME:** 30 MINUTES, PLUS 1 MONTH MATURING
COOKING TIME: 35 MINUTES

500ml/17fl oz/2 cups red wine vinegar
**1kg/2lb 4oz fresh beetroot/beet, peeled
  and cut into small cubes**
**750g/1lb 10oz cooking apples, peeled,
  cored and chopped**
680g/1lb 8oz/3⅔ cups soft light brown sugar
135g/4¾oz grated horseradish

1 Pour the vinegar into a preserving pan. Add all the ingredients except the horseradish, stir together and slowly bring to the boil.

2 Reduce the heat and simmer for about 15 minutes until the apples start to soften.

3 Add the horseradish, bring to the boil and boil for about 15 minutes until the mixture is thick and no excess liquid remains in the bottom of the pan. Stir from time to time to prevent the mixture from sticking to the bottom of the pan. Do not overcook or the mixture will turn brown.

4 Meanwhile, sterilize enough jars with non-metallic, vinegar-proof lids, or preserving jars, so that they are ready to use (see page 14).

5 Spoon the relish into the warmed, sterilized jars. Seal immediately, label and store in a cool, dry, dark place.

6 Leave to mature for at least 1 month before using. Refrigerate after opening.

Mostarda di Frutta

This Italian relish is made with seasonal fruits flavoured with mustard syrup. Quinces and grapes are the most traditional ingredients, but you can use whichever orchard and vine fruits you have. It is usually served with *bollito misto* or cold meats and cheese.

MAKES ABOUT: 1L/34FL OZ **PREPARATION TIME:** 50 MINUTES, PLUS 48 HOURS MARINATING AND 2 WEEKS MATURING **COOKING TIME:** 35 MINUTES

1.25kg/2lb 12oz mixed, small fruits,
  such as apples, pears, quinces, apricots,
  peaches, plums, figs, cherries and grapes
1–2 tsp lemon juice, if using apples,
  pears or quinces
570ml/20fl oz/scant 2⅓ cups
  white wine vinegar
750g/1lb 10oz/heaped 3⅓ cups
  granulated sugar
4 tbsp mustard powder

1 Peel, quarter and core any apples, pears or quinces, and toss the pieces in lemon juice. If using apricots, peaches and plums, halve and remove the stones/pits. Halve the figs, if using. Pit the cherries. Leave the grapes whole.

2 Pour the vinegar into a preserving pan and add the sugar. Slowly bring to the boil, stirring until all the sugar has dissolved. Reduce the heat so that the liquid is simmering.

3 Add the fruit to the pan in batches, starting with the firmest and largest such as apples and pears, and ending with the softest and smallest such as grapes, as the fruit will cook at different times. Cook each fruit for 2–10 minutes, turning in the syrup several times, until tender but not soft. If any skins peel off, discard.

4 Using a slotted spoon, transfer the fruit to a large bowl. Pour over the syrup, cover and leave at room temperature for 24 hours.

5 The next day, using a slotted spoon, transfer the fruit to another large bowl and pour the syrup into a pan. Bring the syrup to the boil and then reduce the heat and simmer for 10 minutes. Pour the syrup over the fruit in the bowl, cover and leave at room temperature for a further 24 hours.

6 On the third day, sterilize a 1l/34fl oz preserving jar, or several small jars, so that it is ready to use (see page 14). Once again, transfer the fruit to another bowl using a slotted spoon and simmer the syrup in a pan. Return the fruit to the pan and bring to the boil.

7 Using a slotted spoon, remove the fruit from the pan and put into the warmed, sterilized jars. Divide the types of fruit equally into the jars, arranging in layers.

8 Blend the mustard powder with 3 tablespoons water. Stir this paste into the syrup and bring slowly to the boil.

9 Pour the syrup into the jars, covering the fruits. Leave a 1cm/½in gap between the top of the liquid and the lid. Fit the rubber band or metal lid and seal the jars. If using a screw-band jar, loosen by a quarter-turn.

10 Label and store in a cool, dry, dark place. Leave to mature for at least 2 weeks before using. Refrigerate after opening and use within 1 month.

Sweet & Sour Cucumber Relish

It was in 1994 that an encounter over a jar of homemade cucumber relish, served with cheese, led to the founding of The Bay Tree. We still sell a version of the original, and it is very good served with cheese, smoked fish and cold meats due to its refreshing flavour and crisp texture.

MAKES ABOUT: 1KG/2LB 4OZ **PREPARATION TIME:** 30 MINUTES, PLUS 48 HOURS SALTING AND 1 MONTH MATURING **COOKING TIME:** 15 MINUTES

1kg/2lb 4oz (about 3 large) cucumbers, thinly sliced
2 onions, thinly sliced
6 tbsp coarse salt
500ml/17fl oz/2 cups white wine vinegar
375g/13oz/scant 1¾ cups granulated sugar
1 tbsp mustard seeds
4 whole cloves
½ tsp ground turmeric

1 Put the cucumber and onion slices in a large bowl and sprinkle over the salt. Cover the bowl and leave in a cool place for 48 hours, stirring occasionally.

2 Drain the cucumbers and onions, rinse well under cold running water and drain.

3 Sterilize enough jars with non-metallic, vinegar-proof lids, or two x 500ml/17fl oz preserving jars, so that they are ready to use (see page 14).

4 Pour the vinegar into a preserving pan. Add the sugar, mustard seeds, cloves and turmeric and slowly bring to the boil, stirring until the sugar has dissolved completely.

5 Add the drained cucumbers and onions to the pan, return to the boil and boil for 1 minute. Remove the pan from the heat.

6 Using a slotted spoon, pack the cucumber and onions into the warmed, sterilized jars. Return the pan to the heat, bring the liquid to the boil and simmer for 5–10 minutes until reduced slightly. Be careful that the syrup does not caramelize.

7 Pour the syrup over the cucumbers and onions to cover. Seal immediately, label and store in a cool, dry, dark place.

8 Leave to mature for at least 1 month before using. Refrigerate after opening.

Butternut Squash Relish with Toasted Seeds

This is a relish packed with Middle Eastern flavours, with a pleasing crunch from the toasted butternut squash seeds. Serve with salads, tagines, kebabs and any chicken or lamb recipes that contain similar spicing.

MAKES ABOUT: 1.5KG/3LB 5OZ **PREPARATION TIME:** 40 MINUTES, PLUS 1 MONTH MATURING
COOKING TIME: 50 MINUTES

1kg/2lb 4oz butternut squash
1 tsp olive oil
600ml/21fl oz/scant 2½ cups
　　white wine vinegar
200g/7oz cooking apples, peeled,
　　cored and diced
200g/7oz onions, diced
100g/3½oz/heaped ¾ cup raisins
grated zest and juice of 1 orange
200g/7oz/scant 1 cup granulated sugar
1 tsp ground ginger
1½ tsp ground cinnamon
1½ tsp ground cumin
½ tsp salt

1　Peel the squash, cut in half and, using a spoon, scoop out the seeds and pulp. Discard the pulp but reserve the seeds. Peel and chop the squash into 1cm/½in cubes.

2　Heat the oil in a frying pan. Add the reserved seeds and cook for 30 seconds or until they start to jump in the pan (be careful, as they can burn you). Remove from the pan and leave to cool.

3　Meanwhile, put all the ingredients, except the squash and seeds, in a preserving pan. Add 600ml/21fl oz/scant 2½ cups water, stir together and slowly bring to the boil. Reduce the heat and simmer for about 10 minutes until the apples start to soften.

4　Add the squash, return to the boil, then reduce the heat and simmer for about 30 minutes until the squash is soft, but still retains its shape. The mixture should be thick with no excess liquid remaining in the bottom of the pan. Stir from time to time to prevent the mixture from sticking to the bottom of the pan.

5　Meanwhile, sterilize enough jars with non-metallic, vinegar-proof lids, or preserving jars, so that they are ready to use (see page 14).

6　Add the toasted seeds to the pan and stir everything together.

7　Spoon the relish into the warmed, sterilized jars. Seal immediately, label and store in a cool, dry, dark place.

8　Leave to mature for at least 1 month before using. Refrigerate after opening.

Onion Marmalade

Is it a marmalade, a relish or a spread? It doesn't really matter as this sweet and tangy caramelized onion preserve is very versatile. Not only can it be served cold or warm but it is great with almost everything!

MAKES ABOUT: 650G/1LB 7OZ **PREPARATION TIME:** 25 MINUTES, PLUS 12 HOURS OR OVERNIGHT STANDING AND 1 MONTH MATURING **COOKING TIME:** 2¾ HOURS

1 tsp caraway seeds
170ml/5½fl oz/⅔ cup balsamic vinegar
1kg/2lb 4oz onions, sliced
¼ tsp ground cloves
½ tsp salt
250g/9oz/1⅓ cups soft light brown sugar

1 Put the caraway seeds in a non-stick frying pan and dry-fry for about 1 minute, tossing continuously, until lightly browned.

2 Put the vinegar, toasted caraway seeds, onions, cloves and salt in a large, heavy-based saucepan and slowly bring to the boil. Reduce the heat and simmer gently for about 2 hours, stirring occasionally, until the onions are soft and browned and no excess liquid remains in the bottom of the pan.

3 Remove the pan from the heat, cover with a lid and leave to stand for 12 hours or overnight.

4 The next day, add the sugar and bring the mixture to the boil, stirring until the sugar has dissolved. Reduce the heat and simmer gently, uncovered, for about 40 minutes until the mixture is thick. Stir from time to time to prevent the mixture from sticking to the bottom of the pan.

5 Meanwhile, sterilize enough jars with non-metallic, vinegar-proof lids, or preserving jars, so that they are ready to use (see page 14).

6 Spoon the marmalade into the warmed, sterilized jars. Seal immediately, label and store in a cool, dry, dark place.

7 Leave to mature for at least 1 month before using. Refrigerate after opening.

EMMA'S TIP Onion Marmalade has many uses to complement savoury foods. A few suggestions include using it in sandwiches; serving it alongside cheeses, pâtés and cold meats; putting it on sausages, burgers or steaks; adding it to baked potatoes; spreading it on a pizza or toasted bread with cheese; or using a spoonful or two in gravy or mashed potato.

Aubergine & Pepper Relish

A relish for those who love aubergines. It is so delicious you may want to eat chunks straight from the jar! It is good served with antipasti, cheeses or curries. Add chopped fresh chilli with the garlic if you like extra heat.

MAKES ABOUT: 1KG/2LB 2OZ **PREPARATION TIME:** 30 MINUTES, PLUS 1 MONTH MATURING
COOKING TIME: 1 HOUR 20 MINUTES

1 aubergine/eggplant, cut into chunks
2 red peppers, halved lengthways, deseeded and roughly chopped
1 green pepper, halved lengthways, deseeded and roughly chopped
400g/14oz onions, finely chopped
2 garlic cloves, crushed
200g/7oz/1 heaped cup plus 1 tbsp soft light brown sugar
200ml/7fl oz/scant 1 cup white wine vinegar
1 tsp ground coriander
1 tsp paprika
½ tsp salt

1 Put the aubergine, red and green peppers, onions and garlic in a large, heavy-based saucepan. Add 70ml/2¼fl oz/scant ⅓ cup water and slowly bring to the boil.

2 Reduce the heat, cover the pan and simmer gently for about 45 minutes, stirring occasionally, until the vegetables are soft.

3 Add the sugar, vinegar, ground coriander, paprika and salt to the pan. Bring to the boil, stirring until the sugar has dissolved.

4 Reduce the heat and simmer for about 30 minutes until the mixture is thick yet still chunky. Stir occasionally to prevent the mixture from sticking to the bottom of the pan.

5 Meanwhile, sterilize enough jars with non-metallic, vinegar-proof lids, or preserving jars, so that they are ready to use (see page 14).

6 Spoon the relish into the warmed, sterilized jars. Seal immediately, label and store in a cool, dry, dark place.

7 Leave to mature for at least 1 month before using. Refrigerate after opening.

Caramelized Peppers

A divine sweet and sour combination of peppers with a touch of chilli. Serve with cheese, fish or charcuterie, as a pizza topping, a topping for bruschetta or on a baked potato. The peppers are wonderful served either hot or cold.

MAKES ABOUT: 1.6KG/3LB 8OZ **PREPARATION TIME:** 30 MINUTES, PLUS 1 MONTH MATURING
COOKING TIME: 30 MINUTES

1 tsp yellow mustard seeds
1.25kg/2lb 12oz yellow peppers
1.25kg/2lb 12oz red peppers
200ml/7fl oz/scant 1 cup apple cider vinegar
300g/10½oz/1⅓ cups granulated sugar
¼ small bird's eye chilli, deseeded and
  finely chopped

1 Put the mustard seeds in a non-stick frying pan and dry-fry, tossing continuously, for about 1 minute until lightly browned. Leave to one side.

2 Cut the peppers in half and remove the core and seeds. Thinly slice the flesh and cut into 2.5cm/1in pieces.

3 Put the vinegar and sugar in a preserving pan and slowly bring to the boil, stirring until the sugar has dissolved. Reduce the heat and boil gently for about 5 minutes until the mixture has reduced by a third.

4 Add the toasted mustard seeds, sliced peppers and chilli, reduce the heat, and boil rapidly for about 20 minutes until the mixture is thick and reduced but the peppers still retain their shape.

5 Meanwhile, sterilize enough jars with non-metallic, vinegar-proof lids, or preserving jars, so that they are ready to use (see page 14).

6 Spoon the relish into the warmed, sterilized jars. Seal immediately, label and store in a cool, dry, dark place.

7 Leave to mature for at least 1 month before using. Refrigerate after opening.

EMMA'S TIP Add an Italian note by replacing the mustard seeds with 2 chopped garlic cloves and adding 55g/2oz/½ cup raisins to the cooked peppers.

Pickles
& Sauces

Spiced Oranges

Spicy orange slices are delicious with roast duck and are remarkably good served with roast chicken, turkey and cold ham, too. The syrup can be used as a glaze when roasting poultry, pork and game.

MAKES ABOUT: 1KG/2LB 4OZ **PREPARATION TIME:** 30 MINUTES, PLUS 2–3 HOURS COOLING, 24 HOURS FREEZING/INFUSING, AND 1 MONTH MATURING **COOKING TIME:** 10 MINUTES

1kg/2lb 4oz oranges
420ml/14½fl oz/1⅔ cups white wine vinegar
350g/12oz/1⅔ cups granulated sugar
3 garlic cloves, finely chopped
1 thin slice of red chilli, finely chopped
1 tbsp whole allspice
5 star anise
½ cinnamon stick
4 tsp coriander seeds
2 tbsp mace blades
8 whole cloves
4 tsp black peppercorns

1 Put the oranges in a large, heavy-based saucepan and add enough water to cover. Bring to the boil and then remove from the heat and drain well.

2 Put the oranges in a plastic freezer container, leave to cool for 2–3 hours, then freeze for 24 hours.

3 Meanwhile, put the remaining ingredients in a large, heavy-based saucepan. Slowly bring to the boil, stirring until the sugar has dissolved. Remove the pan from the heat, cover and leave to infuse at room temperature for 24 hours.

4 The next day, strain the spiced liquid through muslin/cheesecloth into a large, clean pan and discard the contents of the muslin. Return the liquid to the boil, then remove from the heat and leave to cool a little so you can handle.

5 Sterilize enough straight-sided, wide-necked jars with non-metallic, vinegar-proof lids, or preserving jars, so that they are ready to use (see page 14).

6 Cut two-thirds of the frozen oranges into eighths. Slice the remaining oranges into 5mm/¼in slices.

7 Put the orange slices around the sides of the warmed, sterilized jars and fill the centres with the quartered oranges. If you have extra slices of orange left, add them to the centre of the jar.

8 When the spiced vinegar has cooled, pour into the jars to cover the oranges. Seal immediately, label and store in a cool, dry, dark place.

9 Leave to mature for at least 1 month before using. Refrigerate after opening.

Pickled Black Grapes

These bunches of spicy, sweet and sour grapes go well with roast chicken, grilled pork chops and sausages. You could also toss them in a chicken salad, or serve with pâté and hot toast for a delicious first course.

MAKES ABOUT: 1KG/2LB 4OZ **PREPARATION TIME:** 20 MINUTES, PLUS 1 HOUR COOLING AND 1 WEEK MATURING **COOKING TIME:** 10 MINUTES

350ml/12fl oz/scant 1½ cups
    apple cider vinegar
350g/12oz/scant 1⅔ cups
    soft light brown sugar
2.5cm/1in fresh ginger, peeled
    and thinly sliced
½ tsp cardamom pods, bruised
1 cinnamon stick
3 bay leaves
1kg/2lb 4oz/5½ cups seedless black grapes
    still on their stalks

1   Put the vinegar, sugar, ginger, cardamom pods, cinnamon stick and bay leaves into a large, heavy-based saucepan. Slowly bring to the boil, stirring until the sugar has dissolved, and boil rapidly for about 5 minutes but do not let it turn brown. Leave to cool for at least 1 hour.

2   Sterilize enough wide-necked jars with non-metallic, vinegar-proof lids, or preserving jars, so that they are ready to use (see page 14).

3   Remove the grapes from their stalks in small bunches, each of about 5 grapes. Put the grapes into the warmed, sterilized jars.

4   When the spiced vinegar is cold, pour into the jars to cover the grapes, adding all the spices. Seal immediately, label and store in a cool, dry, dark place.

5   Leave to mature for 1 week before using. Refrigerate after opening.

Pickled Pears

Often served at Christmas time, and for good reason, as these are an excellent accompaniment to cold turkey and ham on Boxing Day. Also try slicing the pickled pears and adding to leaves tossed with crispy bacon and walnuts.

MAKES ABOUT: 1KG/2LB 4OZ **PREPARATION TIME:** 25 MINUTES, PLUS 1 MONTH MATURING
COOKING TIME: 20 MINUTES

1kg/2lb 4oz pears, peeled, cored
   and quartered
1l/34fl oz/4 cups white wine vinegar
600g/1lb 5oz/2¾ cups granulated sugar
grated zest and juice of 1 lemon
2½ tsp ginger paste
1 cinnamon stick, broken in half
4 whole cloves

1 Sterilize enough wide-necked jars with non-metallic, vinegar-proof lids, or preserving jars, so that they are ready to use (see page 14).

2 Put the pears in a large, heavy-based saucepan, cover with boiling water and bring to the boil. Reduce the heat and simmer for about 5 minutes until beginning to soften. Drain well and leave to one side.

3 Put the vinegar, sugar, lemon zest and juice, ginger paste, cinnamon stick and cloves in the pan and slowly bring to the boil, stirring until the sugar has dissolved. Reduce the heat, add the pears back to the pan and simmer gently for about 10 minutes until the pears are tender and translucent. They are ready when the tip of a sharp knife can be inserted easily.

4 Spoon the pears into the warmed, sterilized jars. Add the cinnamon stick pieces and cloves, if you like. Pour in the spiced vinegar to cover the pears. Seal immediately, label and store in a cool, dry, dark place.

5 Leave to mature for at least 1 month before using. Refrigerate after opening.

EMMA'S TIP Cloves in particular continue to impart their distinctive flavour during storage. If you don't like cloves, discard before jarring.

Cerises au Vinaigre

In France these spiced, sweet and sour cherries are served with cured and cooked meats, pâtés and Pork Rillettes (see page 218). You could also serve alongside a bowl of olives to accompany drinks.

MAKES ABOUT: 1KG/2LB 4OZ   **PREPARATION TIME:** 25 MINUTES, PLUS 1 MONTH MATURING
COOKING TIME: 15 MINUTES

1kg/2lb 4oz/5 cups cherries
325ml/11fl oz/scant 1⅓ cups
   white wine vinegar
500g/1lb 2oz/2¼ cups granulated sugar
1 star anise
½ tsp black peppercorns
1 tsp coriander seeds
1 cinnamon stick
4 whole cloves

1 Sterilize enough wide-necked jars with non-metallic, vinegar-proof lids, or preserving jars, so that they are ready to use (see page 14).

2 Without removing their stalks or stones/pits, prick each cherry with a sewing needle to help them remain plump during cooking.

3 Put the vinegar, sugar, star anise, peppercorns, coriander seeds, cinnamon stick and cloves in a large, heavy-based saucepan. Slowly bring to the boil, stirring until the sugar has dissolved. Reduce the heat, add the cherries and simmer very gently for 3–4 minutes until the cherries are tender, but do not allow them to burst.

4 Using a slotted spoon, put the cherries into the warmed, sterilized jars. Discard the spices.

5 Bring the syrup in the pan to the boil and boil rapidly for about 5 minutes until the syrup begins to thicken, but do not let it turn brown.

6 Pour the spiced vinegar into the jars to cover the cherries. Seal immediately, label and store in a cool, dry, dark place.

7 Leave to mature for at least 1 month before using. Refrigerate after opening.

Mediterranean Piccalilli

Mediterranean vegetables make this an unusual alternative to the usual piccalilli and would make a lovely summer variation, particularly if you have a good supply of courgettes, peppers and tomatoes. You can serve it hot or cold.

MAKES ABOUT: 1.5KG/3LB 5OZ **PREPARATION TIME:** 40 MINUTES, PLUS 1 MONTH MATURING
COOKING TIME: 25 MINUTES

4 tbsp olive oil
700g/1lb 9oz aubergines/eggplants,
   cut into bite-size cubes
700g/1lb 9oz courgettes/zucchini, sliced
350g/12oz green peppers, halved lengthways,
   deseeded and cut into bite-size pieces
350g/12oz red peppers, halved lengthways,
   deseeded and cut into bite-size pieces
350g/12oz onions, roughly chopped
350g/12oz tomatoes, roughly chopped
2 garlic cloves, finely chopped
55g/2oz/scant ½ cup plain/all-purpose flour
1 tsp ground cinnamon
1 tsp freshly ground nutmeg
2 tbsp ground turmeric
½ tsp dried oregano
1 tsp ground black pepper
2 tsp salt
600ml/21fl oz/scant 2½ cups
   white wine vinegar
175g/6oz/heaped ¾ cup granulated sugar

1. Sterilize enough wide-necked jars with non-metallic, vinegar-proof lids, or preserving jars, so that they are ready to use (see page 14).

2. Heat the oil in a preserving pan, add the aubergines, courgettes, peppers, onions, tomatoes and garlic and fry for about 15 minutes, stirring frequently, until the vegetables are tender. The vegetables should be soft but not mushy.

3. Meanwhile, put the flour, cinnamon, nutmeg, turmeric, oregano, black pepper and salt in a bowl. Add 2 tablespoons of the vinegar and blend together until smooth.

4. Pour the remaining vinegar into the pan. Add the sugar and heat over a low heat, stirring until the sugar has dissolved.

5. Stir the spice mixture into the pan. Slowly bring to the boil, stirring all the time, and then cook for 2 minutes until thickened. Season with salt if necessary.

6. Spoon the piccalilli into the warmed, sterilized jars. Seal immediately, label and store in a cool, dry, dark place.

7. Leave to mature for at least 1 month before using. Refrigerate after opening.

Balsamic Onions

Perfect pop-in-the-mouth-size onions, preserved in a slightly sweet and spicy vinegar. Using balsamic vinegar is more expensive but it adds a lovely rich sweetness.

MAKES ABOUT: 1KG/2LB 4OZ **PREPARATION TIME:** 25 MINUTES, PLUS 24 HOURS CURING AND 1 MONTH MATURING **COOKING TIME:** 5 MINUTES

75g/2½oz salt
1kg/2lb 4oz pickling onions
1½ tsp pickling spice
650ml/22½fl oz/generous 2½ cups balsamic vinegar
1 thin slice of red chilli, finely chopped
½ tsp yellow mustard seeds

1 Pour 1l/34fl oz/4 cups water into a large bowl, add the salt and stir until dissolved.
2 Add the onions and leave to cure for 24 hours.
3 Sterilize enough wide-necked jars with non-metallic, vinegar-proof lids, or preserving jars, so that they are ready to use (see page 14).
4 Rinse the onions well under cold running water and leave to drain.
5 Tie the pickling spice in a piece of muslin/cheesecloth. Pour the vinegar into a large, heavy-based pan, add the muslin bag and chilli and heat gently until almost boiling. Remove the pan from the heat.
6 Spoon the onions into the warmed, sterilized jars. Pour in the spiced vinegar to cover the onions. Add the mustard seeds, dividing equally into the jars. Seal immediately, label and store in a cool, dry, dark place.
7 Leave to mature for at least 1 month before using. Refrigerate after opening.

EMMA'S TIP Don't discard the balsamic vinegar marinade when you have eaten the onions, but use it to make salad dressings with extra virgin olive oil. Drizzle over salad leaves, thinly sliced red onions, avocado, oranges and walnuts. A few drops of the marinade can also enhance sliced strawberries and pears, as well as steaks, eggs, grilled fish and cold meats. You can also brush it over cooked grilled chicken breasts to add a glaze.

Sweet Pickled Beetroot

This is a sweet, spiced pickle, rather than the usual pickled beetroots in vinegar, and the addition of sugar complements and brings out beetroot's natural sweetness. Serve this tasty pickle with cold meats, use in a sandwich or add at the last minute to a duck, beef or chicken salad.

MAKES ABOUT: 1KG/2LB 4OZ **PREPARATION TIME:** 25 MINUTES, PLUS 1 MONTH MATURING
COOKING TIME: 2 HOURS 5 MINUTES

1kg/2lb 4oz small raw beetroots/beets
1l/34fl oz/4 cups red wine vinegar
500g/1lb 2oz/2¼ cups granulated sugar
1 bay leaf
1 cinnamon stick
4 whole cloves
¼ tsp whole allspice
⅛ tsp black peppercorns
1 tsp salt

1 Trim the beetroot tops but do not remove the roots or cut into the skin else the beetroots will bleed their colour during cooking.

2 Put the vinegar and all the other ingredients in a preserving pan or large, heavy-based saucepan. Slowly bring to the boil, stirring until the sugar has dissolved. Reduce the heat, add the whole beetroots and simmer very gently for about 1½–2 hours until the beetroots are tender.

3 Sterilize enough wide-necked jars with non-metallic, vinegar-proof lids, or preserving jars, so that they are ready to use (see page 14).

4 Using a slotted spoon, remove the beetroots from the pan and leave to cool.

5 Meanwhile, strain the spiced vinegar through muslin/cheesecloth into a large, clean pan and leave to one side. Discard the contents of the muslin.

6 When the beetroots are cool enough to handle (wear disposable plastic gloves to prevent staining your hands), cut off the roots and peel off the skin. Put the beetroots into the warmed, sterilized jars.

7 Return the spiced vinegar to the boil, then pour into the jars to cover the beetroots. Seal immediately, label and store in a cool, dry, dark place.

8 Leave to mature for at least 1 month before using. Refrigerate after opening.

A Peck of Pickled Peppers

Not only a childhood tongue-twister, these colourful peppers are an attractive and delicious addition to salads, roast vegetables and pizzas. They will also liven up a ham or chicken sandwich and, chopped and mixed with a little mayonnaise, they make a good spread to serve on fingers of toasted bread.

MAKES ABOUT: 550G/1LB 4OZ   **PREPARATION TIME:** 20 MINUTES, PLUS 1 WEEK MATURING
COOKING TIME: 15 MINUTES

2 red peppers
2 yellow peppers
2 green peppers
600ml/21fl oz/scant 2½ cups
    white wine vinegar
300g/10½oz/1⅓ cups granulated sugar
4 garlic cloves
4 whole cloves
2 bay leaves
½ tsp black peppercorns
2 tsp whole coriander seeds
1 tsp salt

1   Halve all the peppers lengthways, remove the core and seeds, and cut the flesh into 1.5cm/⅝in slices.

2   Sterilize enough wide-necked jars with non-metallic, vinegar-proof lids, or preserving jars, so that they are ready to use (see page 14).

3   Put all the remaining ingredients except the peppers in a large, heavy-based saucepan. Slowly bring to the boil, stirring until the sugar has dissolved. Reduce the heat, add the peppers and simmer gently for about 10 minutes until the peppers are just tender.

4   Using a slotted spoon, put the peppers into the warmed, sterilized jars.

5   Add the bay leaves and whole spices to the jars and pour in the spiced vinegar to cover the peppers completely. Seal immediately, label and store in a cool, dry, dark place.

6   Leave to mature for at least 1 week before using. Refrigerate after opening.

Garlic Pickle

Called a pickle but this sweet, punchy preserve has a chutney-like consistency. Serve it with a curry, or add a spoonful to sauces, stir-fries or roasted vegetables. You can also serve it spread thinly on toasted bread on its own or topped with something savoury to serve with drinks.

MAKES ABOUT: 480G/1LB 1OZ **PREPARATION TIME:** 30 MINUTES, PLUS 1 WEEK MATURING
COOKING TIME: 20 MINUTES

250g/9oz garlic bulbs
   (about 3 large whole heads)
125ml/4fl oz/½ cup white wine vinegar
350g/12oz/scant 1⅔ cups granulated sugar
2 tbsp lemon juice
5 tbsp sunflower oil
4 tsp brown mustard seeds
4 tsp cumin seeds
1 tsp cayenne pepper
2 tsp ground fenugreek
½ tsp ground turmeric
1 tsp salt

1 Sterilize enough small, wide-necked jars with non-metallic, vinegar-proof lids, or preserving jars, so that they are ready to use (see page 14).

2 Break the garlic bulbs into individual cloves and peel each one. Put in a food processor and roughly chop.

3 Put the vinegar and sugar in a large, heavy-based saucepan. Slowly bring to the boil, stirring until the sugar has dissolved.

4 Reduce the heat, add the chopped garlic and all the remaining ingredients and simmer gently for about 15 minutes until the mixture is thick but still with a little liquid in the bottom of the pan. Stir from time to time to prevent the mixture from sticking to the bottom of the pan.

5 Spoon the pickle into the warmed, sterilized jars. Seal immediately, label and store in a cool, dry, dark place.

6 Leave to mature for at least 1 week before using. Refrigerate after opening.

EMMA'S TIP Be very careful towards the end of cooking that the pickle does not become too thick, as it thickens further as it cools and can easily become too sticky.

Horseradish Sauce

The traditional accompaniment to roast beef and smoked fish – they aren't the same without it. Be careful not to touch your eyes while preparing the horseradish, as it can really sting, and wash your hands well in warm soapy water after you have grated it.

MAKES ABOUT: 225G/8OZ **PREPARATION TIME:** 20 MINUTES **COOKING TIME:** 10 MINUTES

1 tsp salt
225g/8oz horseradish root
about 500ml/17fl oz/2 cups
   distilled white vinegar
1 bay leaf
12 peppercorns
1 tbsp granulated sugar

TO SERVE
1 tsp English mustard
4 tbsp double/heavy cream
1 tsp granulated sugar
salt and freshly ground black pepper

1 Sterilize enough small, wide-necked jars with non-metallic, vinegar-proof lids, or preserving jars, so that they are ready to use (see page 14).

2 Fill a large bowl with about 600ml/21fl oz/scant 2½ cups boiling water and add the salt. Peel and grate the horseradish directly into the water to prevent it from turning brown.

3 Drain the horseradish well and pat dry with paper towels. Put into the warmed, sterilized jars, filling them two-thirds full.

4 Pour the vinegar into a saucepan and add the bay leaf, peppercorns and sugar. Bring to the boil, then reduce the heat and simmer for 5 minutes.

5 Strain the vinegar through a sieve and pour into the jars to cover the horseradish. Seal immediately, label and store in a cool, dry, dark place. Refrigerate after opening.

6 To serve, spoon 3 tablespoons of the horseradish and 2 teaspoons of vinegar from the jar, into a bowl. Add the mustard, cream and sugar and stir together. Season to taste with salt and pepper.

Cranberry & Orange Sauce

Also known as Cranberry and Orange Marmalade, this is a tangy, refreshing accompaniment with a vibrant colour. It is a versatile sauce – stir a spoonful into gravy for colour and extra flavour, or serve alongside roast turkey, chicken, goose or duck. It is also delicious with brie and a baguette.

MAKES ABOUT: 1KG/2LB 4OZ **PREPARATION TIME:** 25 MINUTES, PLUS 2 WEEKS MATURING
COOKING TIME: 55 MINUTES

2 oranges
500g/1lb 2oz/heaped 4½ cups cranberries
500g/1lb 2oz/2¼ cups granulated sugar

1 Halve the oranges and squeeze out the juice and pips. Slice the orange peel with its pith into thin shreds, about 4cm/1½in long.

2 Put the peel, orange juice and 1l/34fl oz/4 cups water into a large, heavy-based saucepan and slowly bring to the boil. Reduce the heat and simmer gently for about 30 minutes until the peel is really soft and the liquid reduced by about a third.

3 Meanwhile, sterilize enough small, wide-necked jars in the oven so that they are ready to use (see page 14).

4 Add the cranberries to the pan, return to the boil, reduce the heat and simmer for 10–15 minutes until soft and the skins burst.

5 Reduce the heat, add the sugar to the pan and stir until the sugar is completely dissolved. Return to the boil and boil for 3 minutes.

6 Spoon the sauce into the warmed, sterilized jars and cover immediately with a waxed disc and a dampened cellophane round or a lid. Label and store in a cool, dry, dark place.

7 Leave to mature for at least 2 weeks before using. Refrigerate after opening.

EMMA'S TIP Fresh cranberries are only in season in the autumn, but you can use frozen cranberries instead. It is not necessary to thaw them before use. If you like ginger, you could grate a small piece of fresh ginger and add to the pan with the cranberries.

Bramley Apple Sauce

A delicious everyday apple sauce to serve with a joint of roasted pork, grilled pork chops, duck, or with sausage and mash. You can also serve it as a dessert, or add a spoonful to your breakfast cereal or porridge, sprinkled with a dusting of ground cinnamon.

MAKES ABOUT: 700G/1LB 9OZ **PREPARATION TIME:** 30 MINUTES, PLUS BOTTLING (OPTIONAL)
COOKING TIME: 20 MINUTES

juice of 1 lemon
2kg/2lb 4oz Bramley cooking apples
55g/2oz/¼ cup granulated sugar
25g/1oz butter

1 Sterilize enough preserving jars so that they are ready to use (see page 14). Alternatively, you can store the sauce in plastic containers in the freezer.

2 Pour 150ml/5fl oz/scant ⅔ cup water into a large, heavy-based saucepan and add the lemon juice.

3 Peel, core and cut the apples into chunks and add to the pan as you prepare them to prevent them from turning brown.

4 Sprinkle the sugar over the apples. Bring to the boil, reduce the heat, cover with a lid, and simmer gently for about 15 minutes until the apples are very soft. Stir from time to time to prevent the mixture from sticking to the bottom of the pan.

5 If you prefer a rough-textured sauce, beat the mixture well with a wooden spoon until it is the required texture. If you prefer a smooth sauce, put the apple in a food processor and blend until smooth. Return the apple to the pan.

6 Add the butter and heat very gently until melted. Stir all the time to prevent the apple from sticking to the bottom of the pan.

7 Spoon the sauce into the warmed, sterilized jars, leaving a 1cm/½in gap between the top of the sauce and the lid. Tap the jars lightly on the work surface to remove any air bubbles. Fit the rubber band or metal lid and seal the jars. If using screw-band jars, loosen by a quarter-turn. Label and store in a cool, dry, dark place.

8 Alternatively, pour the sauce into plastic freezer containers and label. Leave to cool and then seal and store in the freezer. Leave to thaw at room temperature for about 8 hours before serving.

9 Serve cold or, to serve hot, reheat the sauce gently in a saucepan. Once opened, store the sauce in the refrigerator and eat within 1 week.

Mint Sauce

A mandatory accompaniment to roast lamb! It is also the perfect solution to what to do with all that mint should you have it growing in your garden, since it has a tendency to grow rather freely.

MAKES ABOUT: 150ML/5FL OZ **PREPARATION TIME:** 25 MINUTES, PLUS 2–3 HOURS COOLING
COOKING TIME: 2 MINUTES

150ml/5fl oz/scant ⅔ cup white wine vinegar
115g/4oz/½ cup granulated sugar
100g/3½oz mint leaves
a pinch of salt

1 Put the vinegar and sugar in a large, heavy-based saucepan. Slowly bring to the boil, stirring until the sugar has dissolved. Remove the pan from the heat and leave the liquid to cool for 2–3 hours.

2 Sterilize enough small, wide-necked jars with non-metallic, vinegar-proof lids, or preserving jars, so that they are ready to use (see page 14).

3 Strip the mint leaves off their stalks and chop finely. Put the chopped mint in a bowl and pour over hot water to set the colour of the mint leaves. Drain well and pat dry on paper towels. Sprinkle with salt and put the mint into the warmed, sterilized jars.

4 When the vinegar is cold, pour into the jars to cover the mint. Seal immediately, label and store in a cool, dry, dark place.

5 To serve the sauce, spoon out the quantity of mint that you require with a little of the vinegar into a serving jug/pitcher or bowl and add a little fresh vinegar. Refrigerate any leftover after use.

EMMA'S TIP It can be a laborious task but, when you remove the mint leaves from their stems, try not to include any stems, as these can add bitterness to the sauce. It is also a good idea to sprinkle a few teaspoons of the sugar over the mint leaves before chopping, as this helps to extract the mint's oils and also provides the knife with a rough texture, which helps to finely chop the mint.

Honey Barbecue Sauce

Sweetened and flavoured with honey, this sauce is wonderful basted over barbecued meats, such as pork spare ribs and chicken drumsticks, or simply serve a spoonful alongside barbecued sausages and burgers.

MAKES ABOUT: 800ML/28FL OZ **PREPARATION TIME:** 25 MINUTES, PLUS BOTTLING (OPTIONAL)
COOKING TIME: 45 MINUTES

1 tbsp olive oil
500g/1lb 2oz onions, finely chopped
500g/1lb 2oz tomato passata/strained
  tomatoes
85g/3oz clear honey
3 tbsp balsamic vinegar
2 tbsp soy sauce
1 tbsp ginger paste
½ tsp salt
½ tsp ground black pepper

1 Sterilize enough wide-necked bottles in the oven so that they are ready to use (see page 14). If using screw-top bottles with metal lids, fit with cut-out card discs to prevent the sauce coming in contact with the metal.

2 Heat the oil in a large, heavy-based saucepan. Add the onions and fry gently for about 15 minutes, stirring occasionally, until softened and starting to turn brown.

3 Add all the remaining ingredients and bring to the boil. Reduce the heat and simmer for 20–30 minutes until reduced and thickened.

4 Transfer the mixture to a food processor or blender, or use a stick blender, and blend until smooth. Return the mixture to the pan and heat gently until hot.

5 Using a funnel, pour the sauce into the warmed, sterilized bottles, leaving a 1cm/½in gap between the top of the sauce and the lid. Fit the rubber band or metal lid and seal the bottle. If using a screw-band bottle, loosen by a quarter-turn. Label and store in the refrigerator. Eat within 3 months.

6 If you wish to store the sauce for longer, follow the instructions for bottling on page 23.

EMMA'S TIP You can preserve the sauce by freezing, if you prefer. Pour the sauce into clean, plastic bottles, leaving a head-space to allow for expansion. Label and freeze. Leave to thaw at room temperature for about 8 hours before serving. Keep in the refrigerator once opened.

Wholegrain Honey Mustard

Everyone needs a small supply of wholegrain mustard and this one is very easy to make. Serve a dollop with grilled steaks, spread on your cheese sandwich, or add to dressings and marinades. Its uses are endless!

MAKES ABOUT: 225G/8OZ **PREPARATION TIME:** 15 MINUTES, PLUS 24 HOURS SOAKING AND 1 WEEK MATURING

50g/1¾oz yellow mustard seeds
25g/1oz black mustard seeds
8 tbsp apple cider vinegar
2 tbsp clear honey
½ tsp ground ginger
½ tsp ground cinnamon
½ tsp salt

1 Put the yellow and black mustard seeds in a bowl and add the vinegar. Cover and leave to soak at room temperature for 24 hours.

2 Sterilize enough small, wide-necked jars with non-metallic, vinegar-proof lids, or preserving jars, so that they are ready to use (see page 14).

3 Put three-quarters of the soaked mustard seeds in a food processor and blend, using a pulsating action, until a thick paste has formed. This will take several minutes. Transfer to a bowl.

4 Add the honey, ginger, cinnamon and salt to the mixture and blend together until well combined.

5 Add the reserved soaked seeds to the mixture and stir together.

6 Pack the mixture into the warmed, sterilized jars. Seal immediately, label and store in a cool, dry, dark place.

7 Leave to mature for at least 1 week before using. Refrigerate after opening.

Tomato Ketchup

Loved by all, this homemade ketchup is less sweet than many commercial products. It is very simple to make and a useful way to use up a bumper crop of tomatoes each year.

MAKES ABOUT: 800ML/28FL OZ **PREPARATION TIME:** 20 MINUTES **COOKING TIME:** 30–45 MINUTES

1 tbsp olive oil
2 red onions, chopped
2 garlic cloves, finely chopped
1 kg/2lb 4 oz tomatoes, peeled (see page 48)
   and roughly chopped
2 tbsp tomato purée/paste
75g/2½oz soft light brown sugar
200ml/7fl oz red wine vinegar
1 tsp paprika
½ tsp mustard powder
¼ tsp ground cloves
2 bay leaves
½ tsp salt
½ tsp ground black pepper

1 Sterilize enough bottles in the oven so that they are ready to use (see page 14). If using screw-top bottles with metal lids, fit with cut-out card discs to prevent the ketchup coming in contact with the metal.

2 Heat the oil in a large, heavy-based saucepan. Add the onions and fry gently for 10–15 minutes, stirring occasionally, until softened and starting to turn brown.

3 Add the garlic and fry for 1 minute. Add all the remaining ingredients and bring to the boil. Reduce the heat and simmer for 20–30 minutes until reduced and thickened.

4 Remove the bay leaves from the pan. Put the mixture into a food processor or blender, or use a stick blender, and blend until smooth. Return the mixture to the pan and heat gently until hot.

5 Using a funnel, pour the ketchup into the warmed, sterilized bottles, leaving a 1cm/½in gap between the top of the sauce and the lid. Fit the rubber band or metal lid and seal the bottle. If using a screw-band bottle, loosen by a quarter-turn. Label and store in the refrigerator. Eat within 3 months.

6 If you wish to store the ketchup for longer, follow the instructions for bottling on page 23. Once opened, store the ketchup in the refrigerator.

EMMA'S TIP You can use canned tomatoes if you need a new supply of ketchup later in the year. Replace the fresh tomatoes with 800g/1lb 12oz canned chopped tomatoes. There is no need to include the tomato purée in the recipe, which is added to the fresh tomatoes to enhance the colour of the ketchup.

Mushroom Ketchup

Dating further back than tomato ketchup, the traditional recipe for mushroom ketchup used to include fish. This recipe uses delicious spices to add flavour instead, and has been given a modern slant by making it a thicker ketchup to serve with grilled and barbecued foods, rather than the thin dark sauce used as a cooking ingredient.

MAKES ABOUT: 600ML/21FL OZ **PREPARATION TIME:** 35 MINUTES, PLUS 12 HOURS OR OVERNIGHT STANDING AND 2 WEEKS MATURING, PLUS BOTTLING (OPTIONAL) **COOKING TIME:** 1 HOUR

1kg/2lb 4oz large flat or
    wild mushrooms, sliced
50g/1¾oz salt
2 shallots, quartered
2 garlic cloves
300ml/10½fl oz/scant 1¼ cups
    apple cider vinegar
115g/4oz/scant ⅔ cup soft dark brown sugar
1 tsp ground allspice
¼ tsp ground ginger
½ tsp ground cloves
¼ tsp ground cinnamon
½ tsp ground mace
½ tsp paprika

1 Put the mushrooms in a large bowl and sprinkle over the salt. Cover and leave in a cool place for 12 hours or overnight. This will darken the mushrooms.

2 The next day, rinse the mushrooms under cold running water and drain well.

3 Put the mushrooms in a food processor and add the shallots and garlic. Blend to form a purée, then transfer the purée to a large, heavy-based saucepan.

4 Add the vinegar and sugar to the pan and heat gently, stirring until the sugar dissolves. Add all the remaining ingredients, bring to the boil, reduce the heat, and simmer for about 1 hour until no excess liquid remains and the mixture is thick. Stir from time to time to prevent the mixture from sticking to the bottom of the pan.

5 Sterilize enough wide-necked bottles so that they are ready to use (see page 14). If using screw-top bottles with metal lids, fit with cut-out card discs to prevent the ketchup coming in contact with the metal.

6 Using a funnel, pour the ketchup into the warmed, sterilized bottles, leaving a 1cm/½in gap between the top of the sauce and the lid. Fit the rubber band or metal lid and seal the bottle. If using a screw-band bottle, loosen by a quarter-turn. Label and store in the refrigerator. Leave to mature for at least 2 weeks before using. Eat within 3 months.

7 If you wish to store the ketchup for longer, follow the instructions for bottling on page 23.

Candied, Cured, Dried & Potted

Crystallized Ginger

Serve these delicate, sweet pieces of ginger with coffee, as you would chocolates, or they also make a wonderful addition to cupcakes, cookies, muffins, ice cream and even your morning bowl of porridge.

MAKES ABOUT: 280G/10OZ **PREPARATION TIME:** 35 MINUTES, PLUS 1 HOUR COOLING AND 24 HOURS DRYING **COOKING TIME:** 55 MINUTES

250g/9oz fresh ginger, peeled
250g/9oz/scant 1¼ cups granulated sugar
100g/3½oz/scant ½ cup
  caster/superfine sugar

1 Using a sharp knife, a mandoline or the slicing attachment of a food processor, thinly slice the ginger.

2 Put the ginger slices into a large, heavy-based saucepan. Pour in enough cold water to just cover the ginger, bring to the boil, reduce the heat, simmer for 10 minutes then drain and discard the water. Repeat the procedure one more time, but reserve the liquid. Measure the liquid and make up to 250ml/9fl oz/1 cup with additional water, if necessary.

3 Pour the liquid back into the pan, add the granulated sugar and heat gently, stirring, until the sugar has dissolved. Add the ginger slices, bring to the boil, reduce the heat and simmer gently for about 30 minutes until the ginger is tender and transparent.

4 Remove the pan from the heat and leave to cool for at least 1 hour. When the ginger pieces are cold, drain well.

5 Place a wire/cooling rack over a baking sheet. Spread the caster sugar onto a large plate and coat each piece of ginger with the sugar. Put the slices on the wire rack and sprinkle any remaining sugar over the top.

6 Leave the ginger to dry at room temperature for 24 hours.

7 Store in a non-airtight wood or cardboard box, between layers of waxed paper, keeping each piece of ginger separate, in a cool, dry place.

EMMA'S TIP If you like you can preserve the ginger in the syrup. Sterilize enough small jars in the oven so that they are ready to use (see page 14). Spoon the ginger slices into the jars and pour over the syrup to cover the ginger. Leave a 1cm/½in gap between the top of the liquid and lid. Label and store in the refrigerator. Eat within 1 month.

Chocolate-Dipped Candied Citrus Peel

Serve with after-dinner coffee or package up to give as a present. You could also make a batch without chocolate to use chopped in cakes, biscuits, cookies and puddings; it will taste far superior to the commercially prepared candied peel you can buy in tubs.

MAKES ABOUT: 68 PIECES **PREPARATION TIME:** 45 MINUTES, PLUS 1 HOUR COOLING, 24 HOURS DRYING AND 1–2 HOURS SETTING **COOKING TIME:** 45 MINUTES

2 thick-skinned oranges
1 lemon
225g/8oz/1 cup granulated sugar
100g/3½oz/scant ½ cup plus 1 tbsp
  caster/superfine sugar
85g/3oz dark/bittersweet chocolate
  (70% cocoa solids), broken into
  small pieces

1 Cut the oranges and lemon in half widthways and then in half lengthways. Using a sharp knife, remove the flesh.

2 Cut each orange skin into about 6 slices, and the lemon skins into about 5 slices each, making triangular shapes.

3 Put the peels into a large, heavy-based saucepan. Pour in enough cold water to just cover the peels, bring to the boil and then drain. Repeat the procedure four more times. The final time, drain the peel well and reserve 240ml/8fl oz/1 cup of the water.

4 Pour the reserved water into the pan, add the granulated sugar and heat gently, stirring, until the sugar has dissolved. Add the orange and lemon peel, bring to the boil, reduce the heat and simmer gently, for about 40 minutes until the syrup has almost evaporated and the peel is tender and transparent. Remove the pan from the heat and leave to cool for at least 1 hour.

5 Place a wire/cooling rack over a baking sheet. When cool, drain the peel well.

6 Spread the caster sugar onto a large plate and coat each piece of peel with the sugar. Put the pieces on the wire rack and sprinkle any remaining sugar over the top.

7 Leave the peel to dry at room temperature for 24 hours.

8 Line a baking sheet with parchment paper. Put the chocolate in a double boiler or in a heatproof bowl over a pan of boiling water. Stir occasionally until the chocolate has melted. Remove from the heat.

9   Dip the flat ends of the candied peel into the
    melted chocolate and then place on the baking
    sheet. Leave for 1–2 hours until set.

10 Put the candied peel in a non-airtight wood
    or cardboard box, between layers of waxed
    paper, keeping each piece separate. Store
    in a cool, dry place.

Candied, Cured, Dried & Potted **193**

Dried Chilli Wreath

Strings of chillies, known as *ristra*, are seen everywhere in New Mexico, where the traditional method of preserving chilli pods is air-drying. Not only is it useful to have a supply of chillies to crumble into recipes, but this wreath also looks attractive as a decoration in the home. Hang the wreath using raffia, if you like.

MAKES: 1 WREATH **PREPARATION TIME:** 45 MINUTES, PLUS 2 WEEKS DRYING

80cm/22in strong but flexible wire,
   such as a coat hanger
about 30 firm, red chillies
about 30 dried bay leaves, optional

1 Wear thin plastic gloves to protect your hands. Thread the wire through the top of the first chilli stem. Thread a dried bay leaf on, if using, followed by the next chilli closely. Continue until you have threaded all the chillies and bay leaves together. Push the chillies close enough together so that you don't see the wire.

2 Wind the ends of the wire together to make a circle.

3 If the sun is shining, hang the wreath in the sun during the day for 2 weeks, putting it in a warm airing cupboard at night. Alternatively, hang in an airing cupboard for the whole time. Turn the chillies occasionally to ensure even drying.

4 When dried, hang the wreath in a cool, dry place. Use as required.

EMMA'S TIP Bunches of herbs can be dried and displayed in the same way. Tie thick bunches of bay leaves, sage, rosemary and thyme with thread. Attach to a wire circle, as explained above, overlapping each bunch so that the stems and wire are hidden.

Dried Herbs

A supply of dried herbs is useful to add to the cooking pot in the winter months, when fresh herbs are not in season. Pick herbs before they flower on a dry day after the dew has gone.

PREPARATION TIME: 15 MINUTES, PLUS 3–5 DAYS DRYING

bunches of fresh herbs, such as rosemary, bay leaves, sage, marjoram, parsley or mint

1 Wash the herbs, if you like, and dry on paper towels. Dip parsley and mint in a saucepan of boiling water for 1 minute to retain their colour.
2 Tie the herbs in bunches using string and put in a paper bag, with their heads down and stalks protruding. Tie the ends of the string around the neck of the bag.
3 Hang the herbs upside down in a warm, dry place such as an airing cupboard. Leave for 3–5 days until the leaves are dry and rub off their stalks easily.
4 Put the bay leaves in an airtight container. Crumble the other herbs before storing in airtight containers.
5 Store in a cool, dark place for up to 1 year. Use as required.

Bouquets Garnis

Useful throughout the year for flavouring soups, stocks and stews, you can adapt your bouquets garnis according to which herbs you grow. This is a classic combination.

MAKES: 1 BOUQUET GARNI   **PREPARATION TIME:** 15 MINUTES, PLUS 3 DAYS DRYING

1 bay leaf twig, 4 thyme stalks, 2 rosemary sprigs, 2 parsley stalks

1 Tie the herbs together with string, put in a paper bag and dry as in the recipe above.
2 Leave for about 3 days until dried. Put in a small square of muslin/cheesecloth and tie with string.
3 Store the bundle in an airtight jar in a cool, dark place for up to 1 year. Use as required.

> **EMMA'S TIP** To make the classic dried herb mixture Herbes de Provence, mix together equal quantities of dried basil, marjoram, oregano, rosemary, sage, savory and thyme.

Dried Apple Rings

The traditional method of drying fruits is in the sun but, since the weather cannot always be relied upon, this recipe uses the more reliable method of using your oven. An airing cupboard would work well, too.

MAKES ABOUT: 225G/8OZ **PREPARATION TIME:** 35 MINUTES, PLUS 11–15 HOURS DRYING

6 tbsp lemon juice
1 tsp granulated sugar
1kg/2lb 4oz unblemished, just-ripe
**   eating apples**
sunflower oil (optional)

1   Preheat the oven to its lowest setting, no higher than 110°C/225°F/Gas ½.

2   Fill a large bowl with 600ml/21fl oz/scant 2½ cups water and add the lemon juice and sugar.

3   Peel (if preferred) and core one apple at a time. Slice into rings about 5mm/¼in thick and add to the water as you prepare, to prevent them from going brown. Leave for 5 minutes and then dry on paper towels.

4   Thread the apple rings onto long thin metal skewers or wooden sticks and place across roasting pans. Alternatively, brush wire/cooling racks with a little sunflower oil and put the apples on the racks in a single layer.

5   Put the apple rings in the oven with the door slightly open. Leave to dry for 8–12 hours. When dry, turn off the oven and leave the apple rings inside for about 3 hours until cold.

6   Put the dried apple rings in a non-airtight cardboard or wood box, between layers of waxed paper, keeping each piece separate. Store in a cool, dry place.

EMMA'S TIP Pears can be dried in the same way but should be cut into quarters, instead of rings, and put on wire/cooling racks. You can also dry the fruits in the airing cupboard. It will take up to 12 hours for them to dry fully.

Moroccan Preserved Lemons

Expensive to buy, yet so simple to make, Moroccan preserved lemons are an essential ingredient in authentic chicken and lamb tagines. They add an appetizing sweet and sour taste that also works well in salads.

MAKES: 6 **PREPARATION TIME:** 30 MINUTES, PLUS 1 WEEK CURING AND 1 MONTH MATURING

6 lemons
6 tbsp coarse salt
2 red chillies
2 bay leaves
2 star anise
2 tbsp olive oil

1 Sterilize a 1l/34fl oz preserving jar so that it is ready to use (see page 14).

2 Cut the lemons lengthways as if cutting them into quarters, but leaving about 2.5cm/1in at the bottom so that they are still in one piece. Open them out slightly and stuff the salt in the centres. Pack into the warmed, sterilized jar so that they fit tightly together.

3 Seal the jar and leave to cure at room temperature for 1 week.

4 Using the end of a wooden spoon, press the lemons to release as much juice as possible.

5 Add the chillies, bay leaves and star anise to the jar. Pour in the oil to cover in a thin layer. Seal, label and leave to mature for at least 1 month before using. Refrigerate after opening.

EMMA'S TIP To use a preserved lemon, cut into quarters, then remove and discard the flesh. Rinse the rind under cold running water to get rid of some of the salt, pat dry and slice or chop the rind before adding to a tagine or salad.

Harissa Paste

This hot, red, chilli sauce is from North Africa and is the perfect partner to tagines, couscous and soups. Harissa paste is made in small quantities, as with its fiery taste, a little goes a long way.

MAKES ABOUT: 175G/6OZ **PREPARATION TIME:** 30 MINUTES **COOKING TIME:** 20 MINUTES

50g/1¾oz red chillies
250g/9oz tomatoes, quartered
1 tsp ground cumin
1 tsp ground coriander
2 tsp caraway seeds
4 garlic cloves
1 tbsp lemon juice
4 tbsp extra virgin olive oil,
   plus extra for covering
½ tsp salt

1 Sterilize a small, wide-necked jar with a non-metallic, vinegar-proof lid so that it is ready to use (see page 14).

2 Cut the chillies in half lengthways and remove the core and seeds with a teaspoon. Keep the seeds if you want to add extra heat.

3 Put the chillies and remaining ingredients in a food processor. Add all or some of the chilli seeds if you like a fiery, hot taste. Using a pulsating action, blend the ingredients together to form a paste.

4 Transfer the mixture to a heavy-based saucepan. Slowly bring to the boil then reduce the heat and simmer for 15 minutes, stirring frequently, until the mixture is thick and no excess liquid remains in the bottom of the pan.

5 Spoon the paste into the warmed, sterilized jar, leaving a 1cm/½in gap at the top. Pour a little olive oil over the top to cover the mixture and form a thin layer, seal immediately and label.

6 Leave to cool completely before storing in the refrigerator for up to 4 months.

7 Once opened, cover the sauce with a layer of oil before returning to the refrigerator.

Thai Curry Paste

An essential ingredient in so many curry recipes, it is useful to have a jar of this tucked in the refrigerator. You can also make red Thai curry paste, which is hotter due to the red chillies packing a more powerful punch.

MAKES ABOUT: 135G/4¾OZ **PREPARATION TIME:** 30 MINUTES

5 green chillies
1 shallot, quartered
1cm/½in ginger, peeled and roughly chopped
3 garlic cloves
2 lemongrass stalks, chopped
1 tsp shrimp paste
30g/1oz coriander/cilantro leaves
grated zest and juice of ½ lime
¼ tsp salt
¼ tsp ground black pepper
extra virgin olive oil, for covering

1 Sterilize a small, wide-necked jar with a non-metallic, vinegar-proof lid so that it is ready to use (see page 14).

2 Cut the chillies in half and remove the core and seeds with a teaspoon. Keep the seeds to add extra heat, if you like.

3 Put the chillies, shallot, ginger, garlic and lemongrass in a food processor and, using a pulsating action, blend until the ingredients are finely chopped.

4 Add the remaining ingredients, including the chilli seeds, if using, and continue blending the mixture together until a thick paste is formed.

5 Spoon the paste into the warmed, sterilized jar, leaving a 1cm/½in gap at the top. Pour a little olive oil over the top to cover the mixture and form a thin layer. Seal immediately and label.

6 Leave to cool completely before storing in the refrigerator. The paste will keep for up to 2 weeks. Once opened, cover the paste with a layer of oil before returning to the refrigerator.

EMMA'S TIP To make red Thai curry paste, follow the recipe as above, but replace the green chillies with 4 red chillies. You need a little less garlic, too – 2 cloves will be enough.

Korean Kimchi

Sometimes spelled 'kimchee', this is Korea's national dish. There are hundreds of variations of these fermented vegetables, but cabbage is most popularly used. It is served as an accompaniment as well as being used as an ingredient in many Korean dishes such as soups, stews and fried rice. Traditionally made by burying a crockpot in the ground, this is a quicker version.

MAKES ABOUT: 1L/34FL OZ **PREPARATION TIME:** 25 MINUTES, PLUS 12 HOURS OR OVERNIGHT CURING, 24–48 HOURS FERMENTING AND 48 HOURS MATURING

500g/1lb 2oz Chinese/Napa cabbage
3 tbsp coarse salt
4 garlic cloves, finely chopped
5cm/2in piece fresh ginger,
  peeled and grated
8 spring onions, finely sliced
2–3 tbsp chilli powder, according to taste
8 tbsp rice vinegar
4 tbsp Thai fish sauce
2 tsp granulated sugar

1 Cut the Chinese cabbage lengthways into quarters and then widthways into 5cm/2in slices. Put the leaves in a large bowl and sprinkle over the salt. Add enough cold water to just cover the cabbage. Cover the bowl and leave in a cool place for 12 hours or overnight.

2 Rinse well under cold running water and drain well.

3 Sterilize a 1l/34fl oz preserving jar so that it is ready to use (see page 14).

4 Put all the ingredients, except the cabbage, into a bowl and mix together well. Add the cabbage and mix well until coated in the mixture.

5 Pack the cabbage into the warmed, sterilized jar, pressing it down to let the cabbage release its juices until the liquid rises to cover the cabbage. Leave a 1cm/½in gap between the top of the liquid and the lid. Seal and leave to ferment in a warm place for 24 hours. The mixture may start to bubble, which means it is fermenting and is ready; if not, leave for a further 24 hours.

6 Open the jar and allow the gases to escape. Reseal the jar and put in the refrigerator to mature for 48 hours before eating. Serve, or store in the refrigerator and eat within 2 weeks.

Red Pepper & Olive Tapenade

This is a version of the well-known Mediterranean spread but with red peppers instead of anchovies. Serve it in the traditional way with French bread and a selection of crudités for dipping. You can also add a spoonful to freshly cooked pasta or boiled new potatoes, or use to make a salad dressing.

MAKES ABOUT: 500G/1LB 2OZ **PREPARATION TIME:** 25 MINUTES **COOKING TIME:** 15 MINUTES

150g/5½oz/1 cup pitted Kalamata olives
70g/2½oz/scant ½ cup capers,
    drained and rinsed
2 tbsp olive oil, plus extra for covering
1kg/2lb 4oz red peppers, halved lengthways,
    deseeded and diced
4 garlic cloves, finely chopped
4 tbsp balsamic vinegar
4 tbsp sun-dried tomato paste
2 tbsp dried oregano
1 tsp ground black pepper

1 Sterilize a wide-necked jar with a non-metallic, vinegar-proof lid, or preserving jar, so that it is ready to use (see page 14).

2 Put the olives and capers in a food processor and blend to form a paste. Leave to one side.

3 Heat the oil in a large, heavy-based saucepan. Add the peppers and garlic and fry gently for 10–15 minutes, stirring occasionally, until the peppers are just soft.

4 Add the pepper and garlic mixture and all the remaining ingredients to the capers and olives in the food processor. Using a pulsating action, blend until a rough paste is formed. If you prefer a smooth-textured paste, blend until smooth.

5 Spoon the mixture into the warmed, sterilized jar, leaving a 1cm/½in gap at the top. Pour a little olive oil over the top to cover the mixture with a thin layer. Seal immediately and label.

6 Leave to cool completely before storing in the refrigerator for up to 2 weeks. Once opened, cover the paste with a thin layer of oil before returning to the refrigerator.

Goats' Cheese in Olive Oil

Keeping cheese in oil excludes air and prolongs the freshness of the cheese. The other advantage is that the oil and herbs impart a wonderful flavour to the goats' cheese. Delicious served with salad for a light lunch or snack.

SERVES: 8 **PREPARATION TIME:** 15 MINUTES, PLUS 1 WEEK MARINATING

4 x 125g/4½oz soft goats' cheese logs, halved widthways

2 rosemary sprigs

2 bay leaves

2 garlic cloves

2 tsp black peppercorns

350ml/12fl oz/scant 1½ cups extra virgin olive oil

1 Sterilize a 1l/34fl oz preserving jar so that it is ready to use (see page 14).

2 Put the cheese in the warmed, sterilized jar. Add the rosemary sprigs, bay leaves, garlic cloves and peppercorns. Pour in the oil so that it just covers the cheese.

3 Seal the jar and leave to marinate in the refrigerator for 1 week before using. Store in the refrigerator for up to 1 week.

4 Serve the cheese with a little of the oil drizzled over the top.

EMMA'S TIP Any leftover oil can be used in a salad dressing, for drizzling over grilled meat or fish or as a dip for French bread. It can also be used again to marinate more goats' cheese.

Sweet Cured Herrings

A favourite dish from the Nordic countries, particularly Denmark, where they are eaten as a starter with rye bread or crispbreads, or as a light meal with new potatoes, crème fraîche or sour cream and salad, or even straight from the jar.

MAKES: 12 **PREPARATION TIME:** 35 MINUTES, PLUS 24 HOURS CURING AND 3 DAYS MATURING
COOKING TIME: 5 MINUTES

6 herring fillets, scaled and trimmed,
   halved lengthways
120g/4¼oz coarse salt
400ml/14fl oz/scant 1⅔ cups white wine
   vinegar
150g/5½oz/heaped ⅔ cup granulated sugar
2 bay leaves
½ tsp black peppercorns
1 tsp juniper berries
½ tsp yellow mustard seeds
1 small red onion, thinly sliced

1 Using tweezers, remove the bones from the herring fillets. You can find small bones by running your fingers along the herrings.

2 Put the herrings, flesh-side up, in a deep, non-metallic dish. Sprinkle the salt over the top of the herrings, cover the dish, and leave to cure in the refrigerator for 24 hours.

3 Meanwhile, pour 200ml/7fl oz/scant 1 cup water into a large, heavy-based saucepan. Add the vinegar and sugar and slowly bring to the boil, stirring until the sugar has dissolved. Reduce the heat and simmer for 2 minutes. Add the bay leaves, peppercorns, juniper berries and mustard seeds. Pour the mixture into a large jug/pitcher and leave in a cold place to infuse overnight.

4 When the herrings have cured, drain off the liquid and pat dry with paper towels.

5 Sterilize a 1l/34fl oz preserving jar so that it is ready to use (see page 14).

6 Pack the herrings in layers in the warmed, sterilized jar, layering them with the onion.

7 Pour the vinegar mixture over the herring fillets, covering them completely. Seal the jar and leave to mature in the refrigerator for 3 days before eating. Store for up to 3 weeks.

8 To serve, drain the fillets from the marinade and dry on paper towels. Serve with some of the onions from the jar.

Beetroot Gravlax

Authentic gravlax is a Scandinavian method of preserving salmon by burying and curing it in salt under a weight for at least six weeks, but this is a much quicker method. Traditionally just salt, sugar and dill are used, but beetroot is added here, which has no preservation properties but looks very pretty. Serve the salmon as a starter with rye bread or crispbread, or as a light meal with boiled new potatoes, dill cucumbers and sour cream. Don't forget to serve with lemon wedges to squeeze over the top.

MAKES: 500G/1LB 2OZ **PREPARATION TIME:** 45 MINUTES, PLUS 4 DAYS CURING

1 tbsp black peppercorns
2 tbsp juniper berries
1 tbsp coriander seeds
500g/1lb 2oz raw beetroot/beet,
   peeled and grated
50g/1¾oz dill leaves and stalks,
   finely chopped
3 tbsp vodka or aquavit
125g/4½oz coarse sea salt
125g/4½oz/heaped ½ cup Demerara sugar
pared zest of 1 lemon
500g/1lb 2oz middle-cut salmon, skin on

1 Finely crush the peppercorns, juniper berries and coriander seeds in a pestle and mortar.

2 Put the crushed spices in a bowl. Add the beetroot, dill, vodka, salt, sugar and lemon zest and mix together.

3 Remove the scales from the salmon and, using tweezers, remove the bones. You can find small bones by running your fingers along the salmon. Put the salmon, flesh-side up, in a large, deep, non-metallic dish.

4 Spread the beetroot mixture over the top of the salmon and rub it into the flesh.

5 Cover the dish and leave to cure in the refrigerator for 4 days. Twice a day, rub the mixture into the flesh and pour away any excess juices.

6 After 4 days, scrape off the curing mixture and discard. Pat the salmon dry with paper towels. Store in the refrigerator and eat within 1 week.

EMMA'S TIP To slice the gravlax, use a very sharp, long, narrow-bladed knife and slice diagonally, as thinly as possible, pulling each slice away from the skin. Greasing the knife with a little oil before you start makes it easier to slice the salmon.

Potted Trout

This is a short-term preserve that uses the method of excluding air and moisture under a layer of clarified butter. You can either store it in one dish or individual dishes, and it makes a delicious starter or light meal. Serve with brown bread or melba toast.

SERVES: 6 **PREPARATION TIME:** 20 MINUTES, PLUS 2–3 HOURS COOLING AND 2–3 HOURS SETTING
COOKING TIME: 15 MINUTES

1 tbsp olive oil
175g/6oz unsalted butter
2 fresh trout, about 250g/9oz each
juice of ½ lemon
⅛ tsp ground mace
⅛ tsp paprika
⅛ tsp freshly grated nutmeg
salt and freshly ground black pepper

1 Heat the oil and 25g/1oz of the butter in a large frying pan. Add the trout and fry for 5–10 minutes, turning once, until cooked. Remove the pan from the heat.

2 Skin and roughly flake the fish with a fork, discarding the bones, and put in a bowl.

3 Add the juices from the pan, the lemon juice, mace, paprika and nutmeg to the bowl and mix together. Season to taste with salt and pepper.

4 Turn the mixture into a terrine or six individual ramekin dishes and press down lightly.

5 Melt the remaining butter and leave for 2–3 minutes to allow the sediment to settle.

6 Carefully pour the clarified butter over the top of the trout to cover, discarding the sediment. Leave for 2–3 hours until cool.

7 Put in the refrigerator for 2–3 hours to set. Store in the refrigerator for up to 1 week. Once the seal of butter is broken, eat within 3 days.

8 To serve, leave at room temperature for about 30 minutes. Serve straight from the terrine or ramekin dishes or, if preferred, turn out onto plates or a serving dish.

EMMA'S TIP Clarified butter has been heated to separate the milk solids and water from the butterfat. The recipe explains how to make clarified butter, but you can use 150g/5oz ghee instead if you prefer to buy ready-made.

Anchoïade

Serve this classic Provençal paste spread on thin slices of toasted French bread or as a dip with raw vegetables such as carrots, celery, cucumber, fennel, mangetout/snow peas and peppers. Perfect with drinks before a meal.

MAKES ABOUT: 165G/5¾OZ **PREPARATION TIME:** 15 MINUTES

100g/3½oz canned anchovies in olive oil
2 garlic cloves
1 shallot, quartered
8 pitted black olives
1 tbsp lemon juice
2 tbsp chopped parsley leaves
freshly ground black pepper
extra virgin olive oil, to cover

1 Sterilize a small jar so that it is ready to use (see page 14).
2 Drain the anchovies, reserving the oil.
3 Put the anchovies, garlic, shallot and olives in a food processor and, using a pulsating action, blend until the garlic and shallot are finely chopped.
4 Pour 2 tablespoons of the reserved anchovy oil through the feed tube and continue blending until a thick paste is formed. Add the lemon juice and parsley and blend again. Season to taste with black pepper.
5 Spoon the mixture into the warmed, sterilized jar, leaving a 1cm/½in gap at the top. Pour a little extra virgin olive oil over the top to cover the mixture with a thin layer. Seal immediately and label.
6 Store in the refrigerator for up to 2 weeks. Once opened, cover the paste with a layer of olive oil before returning to the refrigerator.

Chicken Confit

Originating from south-west France, *confit* is one of the oldest methods of preserving poultry. After cooking, the meat is stored in fat, which keeps it moist and tender. The recipe works equally well with duck.

SERVES: 4 **PREPARATION TIME:** 25 MINUTES, PLUS 24 HOURS CURING, 2–3 HOURS COOLING AND 2–3 HOURS SETTING **COOKING TIME:** 2¾ HOURS

4 chicken legs
75g/2½oz coarse salt
1kg/2lb 4oz duck or goose fat
¼ tsp black peppercorns, crushed
½ tsp juniper berries, lightly crushed
4 garlic cloves
2 bay leaves, torn in half
4 thyme sprigs

1 Put the chicken legs in a large, deep dish. Sprinkle the salt over the top of the chicken legs and rub in well. Cover the dish and leave to cure in the refrigerator for 24 hours.

2 When ready to cook, rinse the legs well under cold running water and dry with paper towels.

3 Preheat the oven to 150°C/300°F/Gas 2.

4 Put the chicken legs in a flameproof casserole to fit tightly in a single layer. Add the duck or goose fat and heat gently until melted. Make sure that the chicken legs are completely covered in the fat.

5 Add the peppercorns and juniper berries and tuck in the garlic, bay leaves and thyme. Cover the casserole.

6 Bake for 2½ hours until the meat is very tender. Uncover and leave to cool for 1 hour.

7 Transfer the chicken legs to a large, deep china dish. Strain the fat and pour over the chicken legs to cover completely. Leave for 2–3 hours until cold.

8 Cover the dish and put in the refrigerator for 2–3 hours to set. Store in the refrigerator for up to 2 weeks.

9 To serve, take the chicken out of the dish and scrape off most of the fat. Heat a large, heavy-based frying pan and fry the chicken, skin-side-down to begin with, for about 10 minutes on each side, until the skin is crisp and golden brown.

EMMA'S TIP The fat can be reused up to three more times to make more *confit* and you can also use the chicken- and garlic-flavoured fat for cooking. It is particularly suitable for roasting potatoes and vegetables, but you can also use it to baste other meats and poultry.

Home-Cured Chorizo Sausages

It was Matthew 'Mash' Chiles' love of continental cured meats that inspired him to produce a chorizo sausage using free-range British pork. The Bath Pig Company started with experiments using an airing cupboard, and is now the largest producer of British charcuterie. This is their original chorizo recipe!

MAKES ABOUT: 1KG/2LB 4OZ   **PREPARATION TIME:** 1 HOUR, PLUS 24–48 HOURS CHILLING AND 3–4 DAYS OR 6 WEEKS DRYING

50cm/20in natural sausage casing, 3cm/1¼in diameter
600g/1lb 5oz pork shoulder, finely chopped
400g/14oz pork belly, boned, rind removed and finely chopped
40g/1½oz Spanish smoked paprika
2 pinches freshly ground black pepper
2 garlic cloves, finely chopped
20g/¾oz salt, preferably curing salt (e.g. Prague powder number 2)
¼ tsp acidophilus powder or commercial starter culture, if long curing
vinegar, for wiping

1 Wash the casing under cold running water, ensuring it is clean by turning it inside out and washing again.

2 Put the chopped pork, including its fat, in a large bowl and add the paprika, pepper, garlic and salt. Add acidophilus powder or commercial starter culture if you are experimenting with a long cure, but it is not necessary if you wish to make a fresh chorizo for cooking immediately. Add a small splash of water to help bind the mixture, and mix everything together.

3 Cover the bowl and leave in the refrigerator for 24–48 hours to allow the flavours to develop.

4 Using a sausage pump, fill the sausage casing with the pork mixture. You will find this easier if the casing is wet. Leave a gap at regular intervals and twist to form the sausages.

5 Tie a knot at the end of each sausage link and attach a loop of string for hanging.

6 Leave to hang in a well-ventilated, dry, cool, airy place, such as a cellar, porch or larder, for 6 weeks for a fully cured sausage or 3–4 days if you want to cook them soon. Do not allow the sausages to touch one another. If there is any danger of flies in your hanging space, cover the sausages in muslin/cheesecloth. Use rings inside to keep the muslin away from the sausages so that flies cannot come into contact with them through the cloth.

7 Check regularly for a coloured bloom on the outside of the sausages (which can form if the chorizo has been stored in a damp place). A white mould should be expected; a black, blue or yellow mould should not be expected and may not be safe to eat. To help the drying process, wipe the sausages down daily with a cloth dampened in vinegar, which will help stop mould from developing.

Pork Rillettes

Originating from the Loire valley of France, this is a classic way to turn an inexpensive cut of meat into a delicious dish. Serve with crusty French bread as a first course or light meal; Sweet & Sour Cucumber Relish (see page 150) goes well with it.

SERVES: 8 **PREPARATION TIME:** 45 MINUTES, PLUS 24 HOURS CURING, 20 MINUTES COOLING AND 2–3 HOURS SETTING **COOKING TIME:** 3–4 HOURS

8 tbsp coarse salt
1kg/2lb 4oz pork belly, boned
   and rind removed
500g/1lb 2oz pork back fat, chopped
2 garlic cloves
1 bouquet garni (see page 196)
¼ tsp black peppercorns, crushed
½ tsp juniper berries, crushed
250ml/9fl oz/1 cup dry white wine
100ml/3½fl oz/generous ⅓ cup duck or
   goose fat, if necessary

1 Rub the salt into the pork belly well. Put in a dish, cover and leave in the refrigerator for 24 hours.

2 Rinse the meat under cold running water and dry with paper towels. Cut the meat into strips about 2.5cm/1in thick, and then in half. Put the pork belly and back fat in an ovenproof casserole dish and mix well.

3 Preheat the oven to 150°C/300°F/Gas 2.

4 Tuck the garlic and bouquet garni under the meat. Add the crushed peppercorns and juniper berries and pour in the wine.

5 Cover the dish and bake for 3–4 hours until the meat is very tender.

6 Discard the bouquet garni. Put the meat in a large sieve/strainer over a large bowl and pour over the fat from the casserole. Press the meat lightly with the back of a wooden spoon. Leave to drain and cool for 20 minutes.

7 When the meat is cool enough to handle, remove it from the sieve and, using two forks, pull the meat into shreds. Put the meat in a terrine or ceramic dish.

8 Spoon off most of the fat from the bowl and reserve. Pour the juices in the bottom of the bowl over the meat and mix lightly together. Pack the meat into the dish. Pour over the reserved fat to cover the meat; add extra duck or goose fat, if necessary. Cover.

EMMA'S TIP To vary this recipe, add ½ teaspoon mixed spice/pumpkin pie spice or Chinese five-spice powder.

9 Chill the rillettes for 2–3 hours until the fat has set. Store in the refrigerator for up to 2 weeks.

10 To serve, leave at room temperature for about 30 minutes. Serve straight from the terrine or dish. Once the seal of fat is broken, eat within 3 days.

Coarse Pork Terrine

Serve this coarse-textured terrine with a fruit pickle such as Pickled Pears (see page 164). You can make it up to a week in advance, and it will improve each day.

SERVES: 10–12 **PREPARATION TIME:** 50 MINUTES, PLUS 2–3 HOURS STANDING, 2–3 HOURS COOLING AND 24 HOURS MATURING **COOKING TIME:** 1½ HOURS

14 unsmoked streaky bacon rashers/slices, rinds removed
1kg/2lb 4oz pork belly, boned, rind removed and sliced
200g/7oz pigs' liver
50g/1¾oz/⅓ cup shelled pistachio nuts, roughly chopped
1 onion, finely chopped
2 garlic cloves, finely chopped
2 tbsp chopped parsley leaves
2 tbsp chopped thyme leaves
½ tsp freshly grated nutmeg
1 tsp salt
1 tsp freshly ground black pepper
125ml/4fl oz/½ cup dry white wine

1 Preheat the oven to 170°C/325°F/Gas 3.

2 Using the back of a knife, stretch the bacon rashers so that they are double their original length. Use to line the base and sides of a 1.5l/52fl oz/2lb loaf pan, allowing the excess to hang over the edge of the long sides of the pan.

3 Put the pork belly in a food processor. Using a pulsating action, roughly chop the pork, then transfer to a large bowl. Put the liver into the food processor and finely chop, then add this to the chopped pork.

4 Add the pistachio nuts, onion, garlic, parsley, thyme, nutmeg, salt and pepper and mix using your hands. Add the wine and mix together again until combined. Cover the bowl and leave for 2–3 hours in a cool place or the refrigerator.

5 Spoon the meat mixture into the lined loaf pan, pressing it down well. Fold over any overhanging strips of bacon to cover the top of the mixture. Cover the top of the pan with foil.

6 Put the pan in a large roasting pan and pour in enough hot water so that it comes halfway up the side of the loaf pan. Bake for 1½ hours until the mixture is firm to the touch and comes away from the sides of the pan. When a metal skewer is inserted in the terrine, the juices should run clear. Remove from the roasting pan and leave to cool slightly.

7 Put a double strip of foil across the top of the terrine and place heavy weights or cans on top. Leave for 2–3 hours to cool, then chill for at least 24 hours until set. Store in the refrigerator for up to 1 week.

8 To serve, leave at room temperature for about 30 minutes, then dip the pan in hot water for about 30 seconds and invert the terrine onto a serving plate. Remove any surrounding fat, if you like. Cut into thick slices.

Cured Leg of Lamb

Curing is still a popular method of preserving in Scandinavia. The conditions must be perfect to prevent the meat from spoiling; start with a small joint of meat first to experiment! The joint of lamb that you use should be cold but don't use a joint that has been frozen, as it will absorb more salt than is desired. Traditionally, cured lamb is served thinly sliced with scrambled eggs or sour cream and crispbreads.

MAKES ABOUT: 2.25KG/5LB **PREPARATION TIME:** 1 HOUR, PLUS 3 DAYS CURING AND 4 MONTHS MATURING

2.25kg/5lb cold, lean leg of lamb
8kg/18lb salt, preferably curing salt
  (e.g. Prague powder number 2)
vinegar, for wiping

1 Squeeze the meat to remove as much blood as possible. Work from the top end and repeat several times. Remove any surplus fat and pieces of meat that hang from the joint. Wash the meat under cold running water and dry well on paper towels.

2 Cover the bottom of a large dish with about 2.5cm/1in of the salt. Add the meat and rub more salt over the joint until it is well covered, massaging into the cuts and crevices. Cover with a mesh food cover and put in a cool place at a temperature of 4–5°C/39–41°F. Leave for 3 days, turning and moving the joint every day, until the meat gives off a clear or pink liquid. Add extra salt if necessary so that the meat is always covered.

3 When the meat has cured, rinse well under cold running water and pat dry with paper towels.

4 Attach a loop of string for hanging. If there is any danger of flies in your hanging place, cover the meat in muslin/cheesecloth. Use rings inside to keep the muslin away from the meat so that flies cannot come into contact with the meat through the cloth.

5 Leave to hang in a well-ventilated, dry, cool, airy place, such as a cellar, porch or larder, at a temperature of 5–10°C/41–50°F for about 4 months. The joint should have a grey surface, be completely dry, firm to the touch but still have some give when pressed with the thumb. Check regularly for a coloured bloom on the outside. A white mould should be expected; a black, blue or yellow mould should not be expected and may not be safe to eat. To help the drying process, wipe the meat down with a cloth dampened in vinegar regularly, which will help stop mould from developing. If kept dry, in air and away from flies, the lamb can last for up to a year. It will become drier and saltier over time.

Index

About the Author

Emma Macdonald, a trained chef, founded The Bay Tree Food Co from her mother's kitchen table, specializing in all types of preserves many of which are featured in this book. The Bay Tree now makes over 150 products selling into independent stores, multiple retailers, gastro pubs and restaurants across the UK. Emma lives on a farm in the West Country with her husband and three sons and is also the author of *Home Deli Recipes*.

Acknowledgements

To all those who have once again worked tirelessly on creating this book, huge thanks for your focused commitment to getting every detail just right. Thanks also goes to my family and friends for supporting me through this journey and making me realize how much I love working with food; without you all it would not have been possible. I hope it will be enjoyed for years to come by many, in the quest for your perfect preserve!

Picture Credits

In addition to those mentioned on the copyright page, the publishers would like to thank Shutterstock and credit the following for their contribution to this title: end papers, Photo SGH; page 4, Gemena Communication; pages 28–29, Lost in the Midwest; pages 62–63, Makasana Photo; pages 88–89, Mark Agnor; pages 122–123, Radowitz; pages 158–159, Neydt Stock; pages 188–189, Leonardo Dutra Luz.

NOURISH
EAT WELL, LIVE WELL

We hope you've enjoyed this Nourish book. Here at Nourish we're all about wellbeing through food and drink – irresistible dishes with a serious good-for-you factor. If you want to eat and drink delicious things that set you up for the day, suit any special diets, keep you healthy and make the most of what you can afford, we've got some great ideas to share with you. Come over to our blog for wholesome recipes and fresh inspiration –

nourishbooks.com.